M000294346

Blooms and Blossoms

Sweet Stitcheries Picked from Nature

Meg Hawkey
of Crabapple Hill Studio

Martingale
Create with Confidence

Blooms and Blossoms: Sweet Stitcheries Picked from Nature
© 2020 by Meg Hawkey of Crabapple Hill Studio

Martingale®
19021 120th Ave. NE, Ste. 102
Bothell, WA 98011-9511 USA
ShopMartingale.com

No part of this product may be reproduced in any form, unless otherwise stated, in which case reproduction is limited to the use of the purchaser. The written instructions, photographs, designs, projects, and patterns are intended for the personal, noncommercial use of the retail purchaser and are under federal copyright laws; they are not to be reproduced by any electronic, mechanical, or other means, including informational storage or retrieval systems, for commercial use. Permission is granted to photocopy patterns for the personal use of the retail purchaser. Attention teachers: Martingale encourages you to use this book for teaching, subject to the restrictions stated above.

The information in this book is presented in good faith, but no warranty is given nor results guaranteed. Since Martingale has no control over choice of materials or procedures, the company assumes no responsibility for the use of this information.

Printed in Hong Kong
25 24 23 22 21 20   8 7 6 5 4 3 2 1

Library of Congress Cataloging-in-Publication Data
is available upon request.

ISBN: 978-1-68356-089-0

MISSION STATEMENT

We empower makers who use fabric and yarn to make life more enjoyable.

CREDITS

PUBLISHER AND
CHIEF VISIONARY OFFICER
Jennifer Erbe Keltner

CONTENT DIRECTOR
Karen Costello Soltys

DESIGN MANAGER
Adrienne Smitke

MANAGING EDITOR
Tina Cook

PRODUCTION MANAGER
Regina Girard

ACQUISITIONS AND
DEVELOPMENT EDITOR
Laurie Baker

COVER AND
BOOK DESIGNER
Mia Mar

TECHNICAL EDITOR
Nancy Mahoney

PHOTOGRAPHERS
Brent Kane
Adam Albright

COPY EDITOR
Melissa Bryan

ILLUSTRATOR
Lisa Lauch

SPECIAL THANKS
*Photography for this book was taken at the homes of
Julie Smiley of Des Moines, Iowa, and
Stephanie Sullivan of Issaquah, Washington.*

Contents

Introduction 5

General Instructions 6

Nest Heart Quilt 19

Gentle Memories Wall Hanging...............25

Wildflowers Needle Book.....................29

Lovebird Pincushion 35

Strawberry Basket Quilt 41

Honeybee Snap Bag 47

Heartfelt Blossom Pendants 53

Needlework Garden Stitch Sampler 57

Blooming Baskets Quilt 63

Summer Charm Pin 71

The Fairy Queen Pillow..........................75

About the Author 80

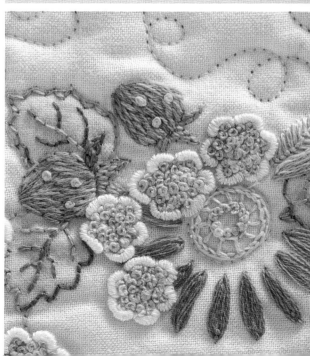

Introduction

I am a firm believer that we need to use our embroidered projects and quilts. We should wear embroidered items, cuddle up in quilts covered with embroidery, and embellish our lives with stitches! In this book, you'll find quilts, jewelry, a pincushion, a needle book, and a pillow—all meant to be used and enjoyed. Browse through the pages to find something that strikes your fancy, then jump in with both feet.

If you already embroider, everything in this book will be doable. There are challenging stitches in a few of the projects—give them a go; they're fun! If you're new to embroidery, you'll find that everything is much easier than you imagined. Don't be afraid to try it all. I think you'll love embroidery.

Many of the projects are tinted with colored pencils. If you've never tried using colored pencils on fabric, you're going to be pleasantly surprised. It's very easy to achieve nice results, even for beginners. Follow the directions and you'll see how simple it is. The bonus? Colored pencils are washable!

Sometimes I feel strongly about perfection. It's a beautiful thing, isn't it? The problem is, not many of us can achieve it. I know I can't. So I decided a long time ago to just have fun and do the best I can—even if it's not perfect. No stress, only fun. Embroidery isn't a competition; the joy is in the doing. When you loosen up and just go for it, embroidery is a joyful pursuit.

I hope you'll love every moment of making the projects in this book.

~ Meg

5

General Instructions

Embroidery is incredibly easy and relaxing. With some basic instructions, you'll discover how simple the projects are to complete. I've always believed that joy comes from doing, and that having fun is far more important than perfection. So, read through this section for general information about embroidery supplies, tracing patterns, color tinting the pieces, working the stitches, and more. Then pick a project and dive in!

Embroidery Supplies

I'll introduce you to the supplies that I've found work best for me, but don't be afraid to experiment.

Fabric

You can embroider on just about any fabric with the right needle and threads. I normally use 100% cotton quilting fabric or linen as my embroidery backgrounds. You can use solids or subtly colored prints that enhance your designs. I love little checks, dots, plaids, and florals. The only fabrics you need to watch out for are ones with painted designs. It's helpful to take a pin or needle to the store with you, and poke at the painted elements of the fabric to see how difficult it will be to needle through. Tone-on-tone elements may also take the colored-pencil tinting differently, which can be really pretty. So it's good to experiment and test some fabrics before you color or embroider.

I add 3" of extra fabric around the perimeter of the embroidered project's finished size. I'm frequently asked why I waste so much fabric. I add the extra fabric partly for the ease of hooping the edges of the embroidery. It is also helpful when sewing a block into a quilt, because the edges will be freshly trimmed and not stretched or frayed, which could affect your piecing. Also, the embroidery stitches can slightly shrink the background fabric. If you cut the background fabric to the exact size needed before stitching, it could end up being too small.

Threads

You're in for a treat because you have so many gorgeous threads to choose from! I love the Cosmo brand because I can always count on their threads for quality and the colors I'm looking for. They're the ones used in my patterns in this book. Most of the time I use Cosmo Seasons variegated six-strand embroidery floss. I love how stitching with variegated floss is like having a whole palette of paints to work with in each skein. You can start and stop intentionally anywhere in the variegation, or just embroider without any planning. Personally, I tend to use the variegation with a little bit of planning for shading or highlights. If you prefer to use another brand of floss, such as DMC, consult the photos of the actual Cosmo floss colors on page 12. I haven't been able to find exact matches, but if you're willing to blend strands of several solids together, it's possible to find suitable alternatives. Just be aware that your results will differ from the colors shown in the project photos.

I normally work embroidery stitches using a 36" to 48" length of floss. That long? Yes! Cosmo floss doesn't tangle or knot like some brands do, so using a longer piece is easier than rethreading constantly. Also, you can lose a lot of the color changes in variegated floss if you use a shorter length.

With metallic or iridescent threads, I usually use an 18" to 24" length. These threads fray and tangle more easily, because they're not smooth. So shorter is better.

Needles

Using the right needle makes all the difference! No matter how great your floss is, if you have a bad needle with a rough eye, the floss will shred and tangle. I use Scarlet Today size 7 or 8 embroidery needles for 90%

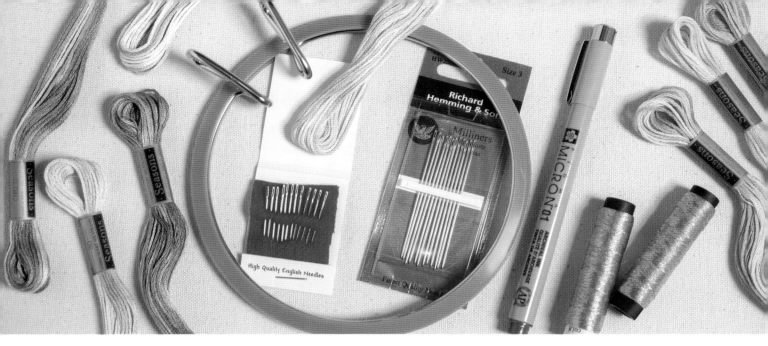

Embroidery supplies include background fabric, embroidery threads, needles, a hoop, and pens for tracing designs.

of my embroidery, and I like size 9 milliner's needles for appliqué and general sewing. (Milliner's needles are sometimes referred to as straw needles.) The Scarlet Today needles are very sharp; they have smooth, dependable eyes; and they don't tend to bend like some needles. If you can't find them locally, I carry them on my website.

Occasionally, if using more than three strands of embroidery floss, I use a size 24 John James chenille needle. It has a large enough eye for thicker thread and makes a hole in the fabric that is big enough to allow the thread to be pulled through repeatedly without being damaged.

Some embroidery stitches, such as a bullion stitch, require a milliner's needle. Milliner's needles are the same diameter near the point as they are at the eye, so you can form a nice, even tube when wrapping bullion stitches. I always have Richard Hemming & Son sizes 1, 3, and 5 milliner's needles on hand. All of the bullion stitches in this book were made with the size 3 needles.

Hoops

I use a hoop! But not everyone does. In the long run, it's about doing what your hands want to do, but if you're just starting out, I encourage you to use a 5"-diameter spring-tension hoop. The 5" hoop will fit most women's hands comfortably, and you can easily reach the center of the hoop as you embroider. Spring-tension hoops are very thin, eliminating hand fatigue. They're also easy to move around quickly with no painful screws to

tighten, and it's simple to loosen or tighten your fabric as you embroider without removing the hoop. I like to embroider with the fabric a tiny bit loose most of the time, but I make it taut for stitches like French knots and pistil stitches (pages 14 and 15).

To rock or to poke—that is definitely the question! I rock, which means I keep the thread and needle on top of the hoop at all times. This approach is much faster than poking, which involves pulling the needle and thread under the hoop with every stitch. For most stitches, it's important to keep your floss and needle above the hoop at all times or else you'll lose track of where you're going! Poking will slow you down, and stitches that involve catching loops will become harder than they need to be.

Tracing the Pattern

I use a brown Pigma pen, size 005 or 01, to trace embroidery designs onto fabric. Sometimes I use a size 05 Pigma pen on heavier or rougher fabric. This ink is permanent and won't smear during tinting with colored pencils or disappear when heat setting using a hot, dry iron. I heat set the ink after tracing; just a couple of seconds will dry it thoroughly. I don't recommend using black, sepia, or colored inks because they tend to show more once the embroidery is finished. Lines made with a pencil will smear when you color over them with colored pencils and rub with blending stumps (see

"Colored-Pencil Tinting" on page 9). Water-soluble pens shouldn't be used with the colored pencil fixative. Lines made with FriXion pens will disappear when heat set and possibly be permanently set if you use fixative. However, if you're not planning on doing any colored-pencil tinting, a FriXion pen works pretty well.

I firmly believe that the "tape your pattern and fabric down to trace" rule is a holdover from the trace-it-on-a-window days. It's best to trace on a horizontal surface, both to save your arms and for accuracy. Pin your pattern underneath your fabric rather than taping the pattern and fabric to your light box. That way you can move the fabric around as you trace. The pins will keep the pattern attached so that the traced lines won't get wonky, and you can trace at any angle that's comfortable.

It's important to trace as little as possible. Any lines you trace will have to be covered with floss or the work will look messy. Consequently, there are certain elements in any design that I recommend *not* tracing. For the patterns in this book, I've marked the relevant stitches as indicated in the bulleted list at right. So for a small lazy daisy stitch, as an example, you'll see only a dot on the pattern, which is where you'll start the stitch. Refer to the project illustrations and photos as necessary while you work through the embroidery instructions.

Use dots and lines to indicate placement, instead of tracing the entire pattern.

- ✦ **Buttonhole stitches and circles.** You'll trace the continuous lines, not the short stitches that come off of them.
- ✦ **Bullion stitches.** Placement is shown as a medium black dot (see below).
- ✦ **Cast-on stitches.** Placement is shown as a medium black dot (see below).
- ✦ **Feather stitches.** You won't trace these at all. Either eyeball the placement or use a basted line, or possibly a FriXion pen line, to show the stitch's direction. If using a FriXion pen, trace *after* heat setting any colored pencil marks or the ink will disappear.
- ✦ **Fly stitches.** You'll trace only the straight centerline.
- ✦ **French knots.** You'll mark a tiny dot to indicate placement (see below).
- ✦ **Lazy daisy stitches.** For small lazy daisy stitches (leaves), you'll mark a tiny dot at the base of the lazy daisy leaf. For large lazy daisy stitches (petals), you'll mark a tiny dot at the base and another at the rounded top end of each petal. In the patterns in this book, dots indicating small lazy daisy stitches (leaves) are black, and dots indicating large lazy daisy stitches (petals) are blue, as shown below.
- ✦ **Pistil stitches.** You'll make a tiny dot at each end.
- ✦ **Cross-stitches.** Placement is indicated by a tiny dot at the center where the lines intersect.

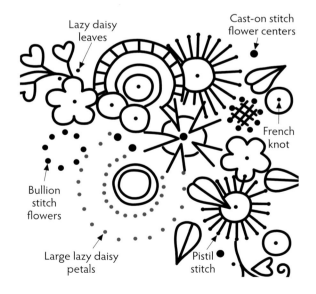

Blooms and Blossoms

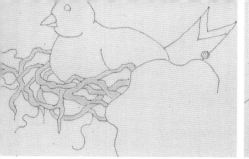

Tint with the lightest pencil, then ask yourself, "What's farthest away from me?" Shade those areas with a darker pencil. The darker shading will make those areas appear to recede. Lighter areas will appear to come forward. It's almost like magic!

Colored-Pencil Tinting

I favor Prismacolor Premier Soft Core colored pencils because they work really well on fabric; however, there are several fine brands of artists' colored pencils available. If you use a different brand, the color numbers and names will differ from the ones I've listed.

I use artist's paper-blending stumps to blend the colors. You'll find both a pressed-paper type and a rolled-paper version; I like the pressed-paper one. These are cleaned and sharpened by rubbing an emery board (nail file) across the tip until the color is removed. Blending stumps are inexpensive, and it pays to buy several different sizes—small, medium, and large. The extra-large ones are too big to do much with.

Keep your blending stumps clean. Any color left on one will mix with the next color you're blending. When blending, you need to rub pretty hard, which will intensify the colors a little bit.

In the project instructions, I tell you when to blend. Usually, you blend light colors first and then add shading and blend it. Instructions are given with this order in mind. You'll occasionally be told not to blend because the design you've added would be blurred and you'd lose the intended effect.

Keep a clean piece of regular copy paper nearby to place under your "working" hand while coloring. This will keep the side of your hand from rubbing on already colored areas and transferring color to the background and other colored areas.

Refer to the photo of the finished embroidery to help with color placement and shading effects. In the instructions, I use "tint" and "shade" when referring to coloring the design. Keep in mind that dark shading makes an area recede, whereas lighter-tinted areas come forward.

"Tint" refers to an allover light color. You can leave some areas untinted and let the fabric be a highlight!

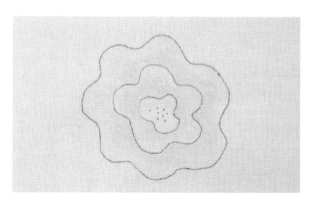

"Shade" refers to adding pools of darker color to show shape or curvature where one element overlaps another.

Video Tutorial

Want to see how I color a design? You can watch a video showing the colored-pencil tinting process at CrabappleHillStudio.com.

Remove Tinting Mistakes

Remove color by dabbing (not rubbing) with removable mounting putty such as Loctite Fun-Tak (the stuff you use to put posters on a wall temporarily). If the putty stops picking up the color, stretch and knead it for a few seconds. Mounting putty also works well for adding highlights after you color.

Always look at the edges of your colored areas and uncolored background. If there are any color crumbs or smears, remove them with the putty. If the fixative hits them, they will bloom and bleed.

Set Color with Fixative

Use fixative to set the colored-pencil tinting. I use Jacquard Textile Colorless Extender. Follow the steps below to set the color.

1. Pin your fabric right side up to the shiny side of a piece of freezer paper. This will protect your work surface from any fixative that seeps through the fabric, carrying color with it. It will also keep your fabric in place so that it can't move around and pick up color where you don't want it!

2. Use a soft-bristled artist's watercolor paintbrush to brush a thin coat of fixative over each colored area. I use good-quality size 6 and 12 sable watercolor brushes with flat ends for this task. Important: brush within the lines so as not to pull one color into another. Do not get the fixative outside the colored areas. When the fixative dries, it will leave an obvious creamy-colored residue. If you use too much fixative, the color can seep outside the lines with it. You just need to wet the fabric, not soak it. You shouldn't have any fixative sitting on the surface of the fabric.

Caution!

It's easy to pull some colors into other areas with the brush. Be especially careful with reds, purples, and black. I like to carefully paint over these areas first, let them dry, and then go back to do the rest of the design.

3. Remove the freezer paper and hang the fabric up to dry thoroughly; overnight is good. If you're eager to get going, dry the fabric with a hair dryer set on high.

4. Clean the freezer paper with water and a paper towel. You can reuse it for future projects.

5. Wash your paintbrush well with clear water. To maintain the flat shape of the bristles and keep them from breaking and potentially getting into your work, never, ever scrub a paintbrush on a surface to clean it! Just dab it sideways under running water and squeeze it with your fingers. Smooth and blot the bristles with a paper towel and stand it in a jar with the brush facing upward to dry completely.

Heat Set the Tinted Piece

You'll need to heat set all the treated and dried pencil-tinted pieces. Press the dry piece with a hot, dry iron for about 10 seconds. After the fixative is applied and heat set, the tinted fabric will be washable. I recommend using cold water and a gentle detergent to be on the safe side. On occasion, I've used a stain remover and didn't have any trouble, but there's always a first time!

Working the Embroidery Stitches

First, unless you're involved in some sort of masochistic embroidery competition, loosen up a little! There's no need to be sloppy and messy, but striving for teeny-tiny exact stitches is really frustrating. And usually you're just pleasing yourself anyway. Most people look at our embroidery and say, "Oh, how pretty!" without noticing that the French knots are a tad floppy and half of the bullion stitches kind of got away from you. Criticism is usually self-imposed, and frankly, if you do have somebody actually picking your work apart, that person is not your friend! I'm joking, of course, but be easy on yourself. Relax, and your embroidery will look better and better the more you do it!

I like to make my backstitches about ⅛" long in the straight areas and a little shorter in little curves. Keep in mind that I wear reading glasses when I embroider, which magnifies things somewhat and I can't see close up without them. So I guess I have no real idea about the length of my stitches! I feel that if stitches are too short, there isn't enough floss sitting on top of the fabric to show up well. And, if the spacing is too perfect, the piece loses the handmade look that I'm going for and isn't as appealing to me. It's a personal preference, and you'll figure out what's right for you.

Let's talk about the back of the embroidery (see "Backing the Embroidery Background" below). I generally use muslin backing, which prevents imperfections from shadowing through to the front. I use knots, leave small tails, and cross over a little bit. If I were going to make something that could be seen from the back, like a tablecloth or tea towel, I'd be much more careful. Waste knots (see below), weaving thread tails back in, and not crossing over even a tiny bit do have their place!

Most of the time, nobody will ever see the back of my finished work (except maybe my quilter, but she's sworn to secrecy). I have had waste knots come out; therefore, I like to make secure knots at the beginning and end of all my embroidery stitching so that doesn't happen. If I cross over from one stitched area to another, I try to weave the thread through an already stitched area on the back and I never cross over farther than ½" or so. If you cross over too far, with use, the thread can get caught on the front of the embroidery, pull, and pucker or distort stitches such as lazy daisies or French knots (see "Embroidery Stitches" below right). Always use your best judgment.

Backing the Embroidery Background

I back all of my embroidery background fabrics, whether they're tinted or not, with white muslin to keep threads from showing through to the right side. Buy muslin of the same high quality as the fabric for your embroidery backgrounds. Super-cheap muslin tends to have fibers and slubs in it, and it shrinks badly. It's just not worth the cost savings. I use 200-thread-count muslin from Moda, which is of great quality and can also be used to embroider on.

1. Cut a piece of muslin the same size as the embroidery background. Lay the muslin on a flat surface and place the background fabric on top, right side up. If you *did not* use a FriXion pen, press the fabrics together.

2. Leaving the fabrics flat on your work surface, baste them together using a hand-sewing needle (I use a size 9 milliner's needle) and all-purpose sewing thread. Knot the end of the thread. Sew long basting stitches

around the edges of the embroidery design and through the center of the piece in a few places. I find that the more I baste, the less trouble I have with puckering. If you baste only around the edges of the fabric, you're not holding them together where it counts and the fabrics will shift as you work, resulting in puckers.

3. Remove the basting threads when you're done embroidering the design.

Thread baste the muslin and background fabrics together to avoid puckers.

Embroidery Stitches

All of the embroidery stitches used in this book are illustrated here. If you'd like to see videos of me making the stitches, visit CrabappleHillStudio.com.

Backstitch

The length of the backstitches can range from about ⅟₁₆" in tight spots to a bit longer than ⅛" in a straight line, or what I call the "straightaways."

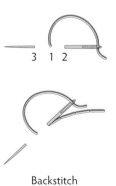

Backstitch

Aqua (5016)

Blue (8054)

Bright Yellow (5009)

Brown (5029)

Brunette (9012)

Charcoal (895)

Dark Blue (5022)

Fern (8016)

Flamingo (5001)

Fuchsia (8009)

Gold (8032)

Gray (154)

Green (8021)

Honey (701)

Ivory (8002)

Khaki (8040)

Light Yellow (8031)

Lilac (8063)

Magenta (8011)

Moss (5014)

Olive (8015)

Pale Pink (8004)

Pine (8024)

Pink (8006)

Punch (8061)

Purple (8064)

Red (5005)

Rose (5004)

Rouge Pink (5002)

Ruby (8008)

Sage (5013)

Sand (5028)

Sienna (8041)

Taupe (8039)

White (8001)

Mauve Iridescent (78-5)

Pink Iridescent (78-4)

Silver Iridescent (78-8)

Yellow Iridescent (78-2)

Bullion Stitch

The bullion stitch is very easy. Don't use a hoop; it would just be in the way. Come up at 1, back down at 2, and back up at 1. Pressing on the back of the needle to hold the wraps in place, wrap the floss clockwise around the needle the number of times specified in the project instructions. Pinch the wraps between your finger on the back of the fabric and your thumb. Pull the needle, then the thread, slowly through the wraps until your fabric folds. Let go of the thread and the wraps. The stitch will flip into place. Go back down at 2 and pull tight to seat the stitch.

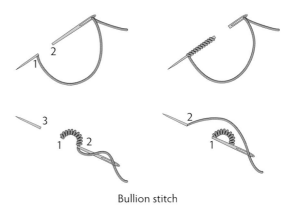

Bullion stitch

Buttonhole/Blanket Stitch

Buttonhole and blanket stitches are worked the same way; the difference is in the spacing. The blanket stitch is widely spaced; the buttonhole stitch closely packed. Both can be stitched in circles, with legs pointing in like wheel spokes or out like sunrays. If the stitches roll in toward the center, tack them down here and there.

Blanket stitch

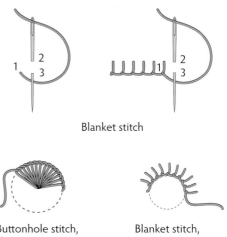

Buttonhole stitch, legs pointing in

Blanket stitch, legs pointing out

Cast-On Stitch (Petal Type)

Remove your fabric from the hoop. This cast-on stitch is built on a tiny backstitch, no more than ⅛". Slide the needle through the top of the X formed under your finger, trapping the knots as they form by pressing the finger behind the fabric against the back of the needle at all times. When all of the knots are loaded onto the needle, pinch them between the finger behind the fabric and your thumb. Do not let up pressure until you've pulled the needle and thread all the way through. A fold will form to the right of the needle. Let go with both hands, and the stitch will pop into place. For help, watch my cast-on stitch video at CrabappleHillStudio.com.

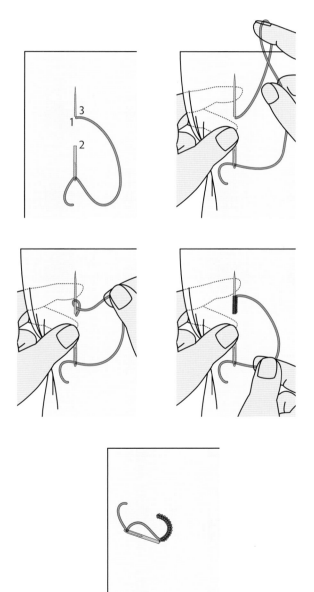

Chain Stitch

A chain stitch looks best when the loops are very small.

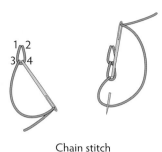

Chain stitch

Feather Stitch

The feather stitch can be used for vines and branches.

Feather stitch

Fly Stitch

The fly stitch can be used to make a tiny stem with leaves. You can use the same stitch to fill a traced leaf shape. Always stitch barely outside the traced line to hide it.

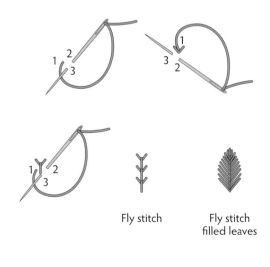

Fly stitch

Fly stitch filled leaves

Lazy Daisy Stitch (Meg's Version)

I like to make my lazy daisies pointed on one end rather than stubby. To make yours this way, come up at 1, go down at 2 (either in front of 1 or slightly in back of it rather than to the side or in the same hole), then rock up at 3 and down at 4. If you pull too tightly, the lazy daisy stitch won't look rounded and pretty.

For a double or triple lazy daisy, make the largest lazy daisy first and then make shorter lazy daisies inside the first one.

Lazy daisy stitch   Double lazy daisy stitch   Triple lazy daisy stitch

No   Yes

French Knot

The key to tidy French knots is to maintain gentle tension on the thread wrapped around the needle, even after the needle is pulled through the fabric. If you let go, the wraps will unwind, becoming loose and messy.

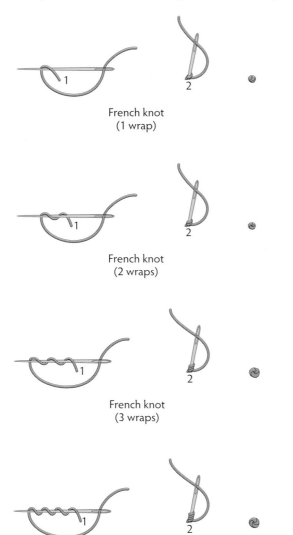

French knot
(1 wrap)

French knot
(2 wraps)

French knot
(3 wraps)

French knot
(4 wraps)

Long-and-Short Stitch

Stagger the ends of these stitches so that they make irregular rows. If the rows are too uniform, they end up looking like satin-stitch stripes. Just remember, if you can see the background fabric, make a long stitch over it.

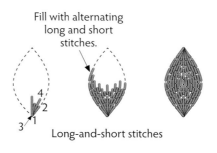

Fill with alternating long and short stitches.

Long-and-short stitches

Pistil Stitch

This stitch is simply a French knot made with a long space between where the thread comes out of the fabric and where you make a French knot.

Pistil stitch

Running Stitch

The stitches that show should be the same length as the spaces between them.

Running stitch

Satin Stitch

If you are using variegated embroidery floss and you have a gap between your stitches, go back and fill in the gap immediately before the color changes on your floss.

Satin stitch

Stem Stitch

The most important thing to remember when working stem stitches is that the stitches should be short and even. Otherwise, your stitching will look messy.

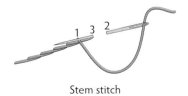

Stem stitch

Straight Stitch

Straight stitches can vary in length and direction, but don't make them too loose or too long.

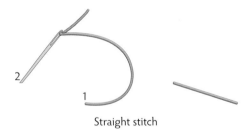

Straight stitch

Cross-Stitch

This simple stitch is used to fill areas (such as a flower center). The crosses can go every which way. The main thing is to keep the stitches about the same size and to fill the area evenly.

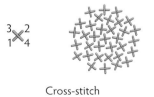

Cross-stitch

Pressing the Finished Embroidery

Maybe you've heard that you should press your embroidery face down on a soft towel so as not to smash the stitching? I don't do that. Coulda, woulda, shoulda . . . but I'm lazy.

1. Use a lint roller to remove any stray threads, lint, and pet hair from your embroidered piece. (I get a lot of stitching help from my cat, Charlie!)

2. Place the embroidered piece wrong side up on your ironing surface and spray the muslin with pressing spray, such as Mary Ellen's Best Press. Press with a hot (cotton/linen setting), dry iron until the muslin backing is smooth.

3. Flip the embroidery over and spray and press the front. I find pressing from the center out toward the edges really helps. Press around the edges of three-dimensional areas. If you have petals that look flattened, use your fingernail to fluff them up. Try to avoid pressing French knots to one side or the other. Just lower the iron straight down on them or press around their edges.

Trimming the Finished Piece

Trimming finished embroideries is among the scariest things I've done in my life. That moment when you wonder, "Did I measure correctly? What if I cut it wrong?" is a big deal after all the time and work you put into doing the embroidery! Out of desperation, one day I came up with a worry-free way to trim anything. All you need is freezer paper, a pencil, a rotary cutter, and a ruler.

1. If your embroidery needs to be 9½" × 12½", including seam allowances, use a ruler and rotary cutter to cut a 9½" × 12½" piece of freezer paper. Double-check your measurements to make sure they're exact and your corners are square before you cut your embroidery.

2. Use a light box, the embroidery pattern, and the freezer-paper template to arrange the embroidery how you'd like it. Make marks on the dull side of the freezer paper to help you with placement on the actual embroidery. Don't be surprised if your embroidery is smaller than the pattern lines. Embroidering usually shrinks the size of the project a little bit.

3. Most of the projects include instructions about where to place marks on the freezer paper—either marking lines around the edges that help with centering, or making marks that show how far from an edge a certain element of the design will be. Arrange the freezer-paper template, shiny side down, on top of your embroidery. Line up the marked lines and press in place using a hot, dry iron. The freezer paper will stick to the fabric.

4. Hold the embroidery to a light source and determine whether you like the placement. If not, peel off the freezer paper, reposition the template, and press it again. You can repeat this process many times if you need to.

5. When you're happy with the placement, use your rotary cutter and ruler to trim the excess fabric away from the edges of the freezer-paper template. Always cut on the outside of the template so that the ruler protects the embroidery from wild cuts.

6. Peel off the freezer-paper template and you're ready to go!

Binding

I use a double-fold binding made with strips that are cut 2½" wide and sewn to the quilt with a ¼" seam allowance. I wait to trim the batting and backing until the binding is attached. For more help on binding, visit ShopMartingale.com/HowtoQuilt for free downloadable information.

Framing Your Embroideries

You've invested so much time and talent into stitching your beautiful embroidery, now you need to do it justice by mounting it beautifully. It, and you, deserve the extra attention that will make the difference between a loose, lumpy embroidery and a smooth, professional-looking piece that you can be proud of.

Choose a frame that fits your embroidery. You may want to go to a frame shop, where an employee can also help you with a mat for the embroidery and may even cut foam core for you (see step 1).

1 Measure the opening of your frame from the back and cut a piece of foam core to that size. Your foam core can be cut ¼" smaller, but you really don't want any more wiggle room than that.

2 Cut a piece of batting the same size as the foam core. I like to use Warm & White batting from The Warm Company.

3 If your embroidery isn't at least twice the size of the foam core, you'll need to sew strips of fabric to the edges. When folded around the foam core, the edges of the fabric should almost touch or overlap.

4 Place the batting on the foam core. If you'd like, you can use a spray adhesive to glue the batting in place.

5 Arrange your embroidery over the batting, right side up. This is going to take a little bit of adjusting and readjusting, so take your time and be patient.

6 Starting on one edge of the foam core, push pins into the edge to hold the embroidery in place. Smooth the embroidery over to the opposite edge and repeat. The embroidery must be taut when you're done, or time and gravity will make it slouch and pooch out.

7 Repeat the pinning and smoothing process on the two remaining edges. Examine the front of your piece to check the edges and your embroidery placement. When the embroidery is stretched to your satisfaction, turn the piece over and pull the two longest flaps over the back. Pin in place.

8 Cut a 2-yard length of either six-strand embroidery floss, pearl cotton, or crochet thread. The heavier and stronger the thread, the better. Using a needle with an eye that will accommodate your thread, thread the needle and knot one end with a big knot.

9 Starting at one end of the foam core, make stitches that are no more than ½" apart, zigzagging from one side to the other. You'll want the stitches to be at least 1" from the edge of the fabric. As you pull the thread, the stitches can tear out if they're too close to the edge. Every few inches, stop to tighten the threads; they need to be very tight. I make a knot in the fabric every time I tighten the stitches. If you need to rethread your needle, make sure you tighten well to that point and knot off securely.

10 After sewing, trim the edges of the first two sides even with the foam core. I cut the fabric even with the edge of the foam core until about ½" from the corners, then angle the cut down a little bit to the fold.

11 Fold the two remaining edges up and pin them in place. Cut their edges to angle them in as needed. Repeat steps 8 and 9 to sew the fabric edges.

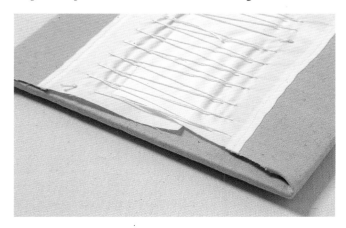

12 Place the embroidery in the frame and secure it with the clips that came with the frame. If your frame doesn't have a back, run double-stick tape about ¼" inside the outer edges of the frame's back. Place pretty paper, wrapping paper, or brown craft paper on the back and rub to seal it to the tape. Use a ruler and craft knife or box cutter to trim away the edges of the paper. This is the perfect place for a label.

Nest, Heart, Quilt

Mama Dove has spruced up her nest with an array of blooming flowers and other treasures. Decorate your nest with this charming dual-sided quilt that features a sweet Basket block opposite the embroidery.

FINISHED QUILT: 12½" × 24½" • **FINISHED BLOCKS: 9" × 9"**

Embroidered & pieced by Meg Hawkey; quilted by Joanie Jensen

Materials

Yardage is based on 42"-wide fabric.

Fabric and Supplies

¼ yard of white floral for Basket block

⅓ yard of pink floral for Basket block and binding

¼ yard of green floral for border

15" × 15" square of cream print for embroidery background

15" × 15" square of white muslin for embroidery backing

½ yard of fabric for quilt backing

17" × 29" piece of batting

Color fixative

Embroidery needle, size 7 or 8

Milliner's needle, size 3

5" spring-tension embroidery hoop

9½" × 9½" square of freezer paper

Ackfeld wire hanger (optional)

Colored Pencils

Colors listed here are Prismacolor Premier Soft Core colored pencils.

Eggshell, PC140

Sunburst Yellow, PC917

Blush Pink, PC928

Pink, PC929

Burnt Ochre, PC943

Light Aqua, PC992

Limepeel, PC1005

French Grey (50%), PC1072

French Grey (70%), PC1074

Beige Sienna, PC1080

Embroidery Floss

Colors listed below are for Cosmo Solid and Cosmo Seasons variegated 6-strand embroidery floss. Consult the floss photos on page 12 when using other brands.

Charcoal (895) for bird's eye

Rouge Pink (5002) for bullion flowers

Rose (5004) for small hearts

Sage (5013) for daisy center

Moss (5014) for leaves and vines

Aqua (5016) for rope trim

Sand (5028) for bird's body, stripes, and bottom of large heart

Brown (5029) for twigs

White (8001) for lace trim

Pink (8006) for scallop lace

Magenta (8011) for flower petals

Light Yellow (8031) for bird's beak and flower centers

Punch (8061) for flowers

Purple (8064) for flowers

Brunette (9012) for twigs

Cutting

From the white floral, cut:

1 fussy-cut square, 6⅞" × 6⅞"; cut in half diagonally to yield 2 large triangles (1 is extra)

1 square, 3⅞" × 3⅞"; cut in half diagonally to yield 2 small triangles (1 is extra)

7 squares, 2⅜" × 2⅜"

2 rectangles, 2" × 6½"

2 squares, 2" × 2"

From the pink floral, cut:

10 squares, 2⅜" × 2⅜"; cut 3 of the squares in half diagonally to yield 6 triangles

3 strips, 2½" × 42"

From the green floral, cut:

1 strip, 3½" × 12½"

2 strips, 2" × 12½"

4 strips, 2" × 9½"

Tracing and Tinting the Design

Refer to "General Instructions" on page 6 for in-depth information on tracing, tinting, and embroidering the design.

1 Center and trace the pattern on page 24 onto the right side of the cream square.

2 Using the colored pencils, color the design in the following order, referring to the photo on page 21 as needed.

- **Eggshell:** Shade every other stripe on the bottom of the heart; blend.

- **Pink:** Sharpen the pencil and draw little circles within the top area of the large heart. Dull the pencil a little bit and fill in around the circles to make a polka-dot pattern at the top of the heart. Shade the scalloped lace edge. Blend the Pink, taking care not to blend into the white dots at the top of the heart.

- **Sunburst Yellow:** Tint the center of the rose (under the French knot symbols) and the bird's beak; blend.

- **Blush Pink:** Shade the rose; blend.

- **Light Aqua:** Shade the rope trim; blend.

- **Beige Sienna:** Tint the twigs in the nest; blend.

- **Burnt Ochre:** Shade the twigs and the bird's beak; blend.

- **Limepeel:** Tint the large leaves and the center circle of the large daisy; blend.

- **Blush Pink:** Lightly shade the bird's cheek and breast; blend.

- **Beige Sienna and French Grey (50%):** Shade the bird's body; blend, but be careful not to blend out the pink on the cheek and breast.

- **French Grey (70%):** Shade the bird's body further; blend.

3 Apply fixative to the colored design. Let dry and then heat set. Baste the muslin square to the wrong side of the cream square.

Embroidering the Design

Use two strands of floss and the embroidery needle to stitch the design unless otherwise indicated. Stitch the design in the order given below.

- **Sand:** Backstitch the bird's body and the outer edges and stripes on the lower half of the heart.

- **White:** Backstitch the inner scallops of the lace.

- **Pink:** Backstitch the scalloped lace edge. Make two-wrap French knots along the edge of the lace.

- **Aqua:** Backstitch the rope trim.

- **Moss:** Work double lazy daisy stitches for the small leaves and fill the large leaves with tightly spaced fly stitches. Backstitch the vines.

- **Magenta:** Blanket-stitch the edges of the rose petals.

- **Light Yellow:** Backstitch the bird's beak.

- **Charcoal:** Satin stitch the bird's eye.

- **Brown:** Backstitch the lighter twigs in the nest, referring to the photo on page 21.

- **Brunette:** Backstitch the remainder of the twigs. Use one strand to backstitch the tendrils extending from the nest.

- **Rose:** Satin stitch the little hearts.

- **Light Yellow:** Work a tiny chain stitch around the small, innermost ring of the daisy.

- **Sage:** Work a tiny chain stitch around the two outer rings of the daisy, and a feather stitch inside the smaller ring.

- **Rouge Pink:** Use three strands of floss and the milliner's needle to make 18-wrap bullion stitch petals for the flower below the rose.

- **Purple:** Using three strands, make five 16-knot cast-on stitch petals around each of the three large dots around the rose.

- **Light Yellow:** Make a three-wrap French knot at the center of each purple flower.

- **Punch:** Make 10 double lazy daisy stitches around the concentric circles of the daisy, working from dot to dot.

- **Light Yellow:** Fill the centers of the rose, daisy, and bullion flower with three-wrap French knots.

Making the Basket Block

Use ¼" seam allowances. Press the seam allowances as indicated by the arrows.

1 Mark a diagonal line from corner to corner on the wrong side of the white floral 2⅜" squares. Layer a marked square on a pink square, right sides together. Sew ¼" from both sides of the drawn line. Cut the unit apart on the marked line to make two half-square-triangle units measuring 2" square, including seam allowances. Repeat to make a total of 14 units (one is extra).

Make 14 units,
2" × 2".

2 Arrange five half-square-triangle units, four pink triangles, and one white 2" square in four rows, noting the orientation of the units. Sew the pieces into rows. Join the rows. Add a white large triangle to the long diagonal edge of the pieced section. The basket-center unit should measure 6½" square, including the seam allowances.

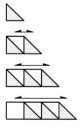

Make 1 unit,
6½" × 6½".

4 Sew the basket-top units to the right and top edges of the basket-center unit. The basket unit should measure 8" square, including the seam allowances.

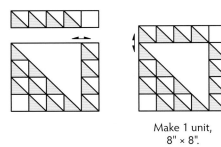

Make 1 unit,
8" × 8".

5 Sew each of the remaining pink triangles to the end of a white 2" × 6½" rectangle as shown for the basket feet.

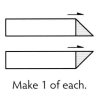

Make 1 of each.

6 Join the basket-feet units to the left and bottom edges of the basket unit.

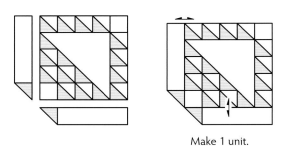

Make 1 unit.

7 Sew a white small triangle to the bottom-left corner of the unit from step 6 to complete the block. The block should measure 9½" square, including the seam allowances.

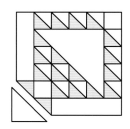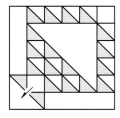

Basket block.
Make 1 block,
9½" × 9½".

3 Join four half-square-triangle units, noting their orientation, to make a basket-top unit measuring 2" × 6½", including seam allowances. Repeat to make a mirror-image unit, adding the remaining white 2" square to the right end. This unit should measure 2" × 8", including seam allowances.

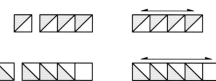

Make 1 of each.

Assembling the Quilt Top

1 Refer to "Pressing the Finished Embroidery" on page 16 to press the embroidered square.

2 Refer to "Trimming the Finished Piece" on page 16 to mark lines 1" in from all four edges of the freezer-paper square. Then mark lines 1½" in from all four edges. The marked lines will help you center and arrange your design. Trim the embroidery to 9½" square and remove the freezer-paper template.

3 Sew green 2" × 9½" strips to the sides of the embroidery and Basket block as shown in the quilt assembly diagram. Sew the green 3½" × 12½" strip between the blocks, noting the orientation of the blocks. Sew green 2" × 12½" strips to opposite ends of the quilt. The quilt top should measure 12½" × 24½".

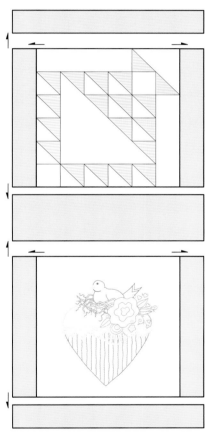

Quilt assembly

Finishing the Quilt

For help with any of the following steps, go to ShopMartingale.com/HowtoQuilt for free, downloadable instructions.

1 Layer the quilt top with batting and backing. Baste the layers together.

2 Hand or machine quilt as desired. The quilt shown is machine quilted with curved lines in the center of the Basket block and a stipple design in the outer edges of the Basket block. The embroidery block is quilted with pebbles in the background; the embroidered area is left unquilted. Loops are quilted between the blocks, and feathers are quilted throughout the border.

3 Use the pink 2½"-wide strips to make binding, and then attach the binding to the quilt.

Nest Heart Quilt

Gentle Memories Wall Hanging

How to turn a teeny-tiny embroidered piece into something that makes a really big impression? Frame a bit of Scherenschnitte (which means "scissor cuts" in German) paper cutting. If you've never tried this type of paper cutting, you're in for a treat, because it's very easy and looks incredibly cool. I used a page from an old book, stained it with tea, and tinted it with watercolor pencils.

FINISHED SIZE: 10" × 8" (without frame)

Made by Meg Hawkey

Materials

Check your supplies to see what you already have and what's needed.

Fabric and Supplies

16" × 20" rectangle of oat linen for background

7" × 7" square of white solid for embroidery background

7" × 7" square of white muslin for embroidery backing

3" × 3" square of white wool felt for heart backing

Page from old book or copy of an old book page (see "Tea Staining the Book Page" on page 27)

Light box

FriXion pen or a sharp pencil

Sharp paper-cutting scissors

Pink and yellow watercolor pencils (I used Derwent.)

Small, round watercolor paintbrush

Brown Pigma pen, size 01

Color fixative

5" spring-tension embroidery hoop

Embroidery needle, size 7

Aleene's Tacky glue

Framing Materials

To frame your design like the project shown, you will need the following. (See "Framing Your Embroideries" on page 17.)

Frame with 8" × 10" opening

8" × 10" piece of foam core

8" × 10" piece of batting

Pins with large heads

Heavy thread, such as crochet thread, or 6 strands of embroidery floss

Milliner's needle, size 1, or chenille needle

Strips of fabric to enlarge your embroidery (optional)

Colored Pencils

Colors listed below are Prismacolor Premier Soft Core colored pencils.

Limepeel, PC1005

Kelly Green, PC1096

Blush Pink, PC928

Pink, PC929

Embroidery Floss

Colors listed below are for Cosmo Seasons variegated 6-strand embroidery floss. Consult the floss photos on page 12 when using other brands.

Sage (5013) for leaves

Moss (5014) for vine

Light Yellow (8031) for flower center and outer edge of heart

Punch (8061) for flower

Tracing and Tinting the Design

Refer to "General Instructions" on page 6 for in-depth information on tracing, tinting, and embroidering the design. Patterns for paper cutting and embroidery are on page 28.

1 Fold the book page in half, right sides together. Unfold the page. Using a light box, align the fold line on the book page with the fold line of the paper-cutting pattern.

2 Use a FriXion pen or sharp pencil to trace around the design. The FriXion pen works well because the lines will disappear when pressed with a hot iron.

3 Carefully hold the two layers of the folded paper together as you cut out the design on the traced lines. If you used a FriXion pen, press to remove the markings.

4 Using a pink watercolor pencil, lightly color the tips of the leaves and breasts of the birds. Use a yellow watercolor pencil to lightly color the flowers. Then lightly brush the leaves, birds, and flowers with a wet watercolor brush to slightly soften and spread the colors. Let dry completely.

Tea Staining the Book Page

If you want to tea stain the book page to make it look old, soak two bags of black tea in ½ cup of hot water for five minutes. When the tea is your desired strength, dip a paintbrush into the tea and brush it onto the book page. Let dry thoroughly.

5 Use a brown Pigma pen to trace the embroidery heart design onto the center of the white solid square. Make sure *not* to draw the lines all the way to the edges of the heart. The heart will be cut out, and if the embroidery goes to the edge or beyond, the threads will be cut.

6 Using the colored pencils, color the design in the following order, referring to the photo on page 28 as needed.

- **Limepeel:** Tint the leaves. Shade them with Kelly Green; blend.
- **Blush Pink:** Tint the flower petals. Shade them with Pink; blend.

7 Apply fixative to the colored design. Let dry and then heat set. Baste the muslin square to the wrong side of the embroidered square.

Embroidering and Assembling the Heart

Use two strands of floss and the embroidery needle to stitch the design unless otherwise indicated.

1 Use Moss floss to backstitch the vine.

2 Use Sage floss to backstitch the top leaf. Fill the other leaf with closely spaced fly stitches.

3 Use Punch floss to make a tiny chain stitch around the flower petals.

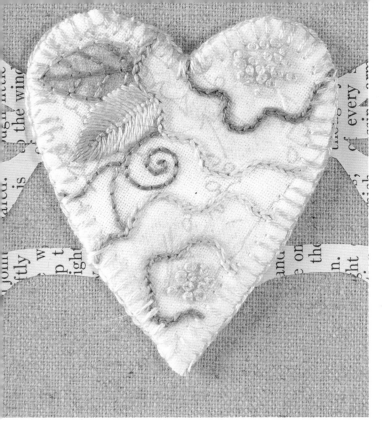

3 Use tacky glue to adhere the paper-cut design to the linen. Place most of the glue in the center where the heart will cover it up. Use tiny dabs of glue to secure the bird, flowers, and leaves.

4 Glue the embroidered heart in place. The cutouts in the paper will allow everything to adhere really well. Let dry completely.

5 Place the embroidery in the frame and secure it with the clips that came with the frame.

4 Use Light Yellow floss and two-wrap French knots to fill the centers of the flowers.

5 Press the completed embroidery. Center the stitched heart on the square of white wool felt. Hand baste the embroidery to the wool felt. Cut around the marked edge of the heart.

6 Using two strands of Light Yellow floss, blanket stitch around the edges of the heart, stitching through all of the layers. Remove the basting stitches.

Framing the Design

1 Place the batting on top of the foam core. Center the oat linen on top of the batting. Pin in place, making sure the linen is tight and smooth. Stretch the linen over the foam core/batting as described in "Framing Your Embroideries" on page 17.

2 Arrange the paper-cut design and embroidered heart on the linen. Leave the paper in place, but remove the heart.

Place on fold.

Paper-cutting pattern

Embroidery pattern

Wildflowers Needle Book

I originally designed this embroidery for a class held at a beautiful resort next to the Pacific Ocean on the Oregon coast. The flowers remind me of the lush gardens and wildflowers blooming along every road. After I got home, I decided that these motifs were the perfect size for a large needle book!

FINISHED SIZE: 4½" × 5½" (closed); 4½" × 10⅝" (open)

Made by Meg Hawkey

Materials

Yardage is based on 42"-wide fabric. Check your supplies to see what you already have and what's needed.

Fabric and Supplies

10" × 12" rectangle of cream print for embroidery background

10" × 12" rectangle of white muslin for embroidery backing

4" × 10⅝" rectangle of pink print for pocket

9" × 12" rectangle of white muslin for pocket backing

4½" × 5½" rectangle of pink print for back cover

4½" × 10⅝" rectangle of pink floral for lining

3½" × 6" rectangle of cream floral for needle page decoration

4" × 9¾" rectangle of cream wool felt for needle pages

2½" × 42" strip of aqua floral for binding

4½" × 10⅝" piece of batting

2 mother-of-pearl buttons, ½" diameter

Sequins and glass beads (optional)

Pink covered-elastic hair tie

Brown Pigma pen, size 005 or 01

FriXion pen

Embroidery needle, size 7 or 8

Milliner's needle, size 3

5" spring-tension embroidery hoop

4½" × 5⅝" piece of freezer paper

Rotary cutter and pinking blade

Embroidery Floss

Colors listed below are for Cosmo Seasons variegated 6-strand embroidery floss. Consult the floss photos on page 12 when using other brands.

Flamingo (5001) for five-petal and small circle flowers

Rose (5004) for hearts

Moss (5014) for leaves and vines

White (8001) for phlox flower

Pink (8006) for large circle flower and phlox flower

Ruby (8008) for bullion and cast-on flowers

Fern (8016) for flower center, pistil flower, and cast-on flower

Light Yellow (8031) for flower centers and cast-on flower

Sienna (8041) for letters

Punch (8061) for small circle flowers and lazy daisy flower

Lilac (8063) for large circle flower and cast-on flower

Instant Aging

To give the needle pages an antique feel, you can coffee-stain the wool felt by spraying it with and dipping it in brewed coffee. Air dry. Wait until after staining to cut out the pieces, because dyeing can distort the wool felt.

Embroidering the Cover Design

Refer to "General Instructions" on page 6 for more in-depth information on tracing and embroidering the needle book. Use two strands of floss and the embroidery needle to stitch the design unless otherwise indicated.

Center and trace the cover pattern on page 34 onto the right side of the cream rectangle using the brown Pigma pen. Baste the muslin rectangle to the wrong side of the cream rectangle.

- **Moss:** Backstitch the vine and make double lazy daisy stitches for the small leaves. Fill the large leaves with fly stitches and then backstitch around each leaf.

- **Lilac:** Make the long straight stitches of the outer ring. Work a tiny chain stitch around the outer edge of this ring. Using pink floss and starting on the inner edge of the inner ring, make blanket stitches with the legs pointing out. Backstitch around the outer edge of this ring.

- **Light Yellow:** Work a tiny chain stitch for the center ring of the daisy and make cross-stitches in the center of the bullion flower and phlox flower.

- **Flamingo:** Blanket-stitch the five-petal flowers first and then stitch the small circle flowers. It's fine for the circle flowers to overlap.

- **Fern:** Make three rows of tiny chain stitches to fill the ring between the circles.

- **Punch:** Make the medium blanket-stitch circle flowers. Where the flower and leaf overlap next to the daisy, work little satin stitches until you get to the other side. Make double lazy daisy petals between the dots around the daisy.

- **Rose:** Satin stitch the hearts.

- **White:** Starting in the center, fill the phlox petals with long-and-short stitches up to the line. End with a jagged edge.

- **Pink:** Fill the outer area of the phlox petals with long-and-short stitches. The outer edges of the petals should be jagged.

- **Fern:** Make three-wrap pistil stitches from the outer edge of each medium blanket-stitch circle flower to the dots.

- **Ruby:** Use a milliner's needle to work from dot to dot, making 16-wrap bullion stitches for the flower on the right. For the flower on the left, work from dot to dot, making 18-wrap bullion stitches. Then, for the flower on the left, make another ring of bullion stitches inside the first, offsetting the stitches with the previous ones.

- **Flamingo:** Fill the double bullion flower with three-wrap French knots.

- **Light Yellow:** Make three-wrap French knots for centers of all the circle, five-petal, and double bullion flowers.

- **Sienna:** Use backstitch to embroider your name or a verse (see photo above). To dot an *i* or *j*, make a one-wrap French knot.

- **Ruby, Fern, Light Yellow, and Lilac:** For the cast-on flowers, make one four-petal flower from each color, using 16-knot cast-on stitches. Make three-wrap French knots for flower centers.

- **Sequins and beads:** Remove all the basting stitches and press well. To add a few scattered sequins and beads, sew up through a sequin (cupped side up to catch the light), then through a bead. Sew back down through the sequin and knot off on the back. The bead will keep the sequin in place.

Embroidering the Pocket Design

Use two strands of floss and the embroidery needle to stitch the design.

1 Trace the pocket pattern on page 34 onto the left end of the pink print 4" × 10⅝" rectangle. The bottom edge of the lower circle flower should be ¾" from the bottom edge of the rectangle. The left side of the vine should be about ¾" from the left edge of the rectangle. Baste the muslin 9" × 12" rectangle to the wrong side of the pink rectangle.

2 Stitch the design in the order given below.

- **Moss:** Backstitch the vine and make double lazy daisy leaves.
- **Sienna:** Backstitch the word *Needles*.
- **Rose:** Satin stitch the hearts.
- **Punch:** Make blanket-stitched circle flowers.
- **Light Yellow:** Make a two-wrap French knot for the center of each flower.

3 Remove the basting threads and press the embroidered rectangle. Trim the excess muslin even with the edges of the pink rectangle.

Making the Needle Book

1 Referring to "Trimming the Finished Piece" on page 16, trim the cover embroidery to 4½" × 5⅝" and remove the freezer-paper template.

2 Sew the pink print 4½" × 5½" rectangle to the left side of the cover embroidery to make the exterior cover of the needle book. The cover should measure 4½" × 10⅝", including seam allowances.

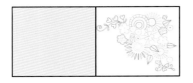

3 Fold the embroidered pocket in half lengthwise and press the fold. Place the pocket along the bottom edge of the pink floral 4½" × 10⅝" lining rectangle. Machine stitch about ⅛" from the bottom edge to make the lining/pocket.

4 Place the exterior cover wrong side up, with the embroidered cover on the left. Center the batting on top of the exterior cover. Center the lining/pocket right side up on top of the batting. Pin baste the layers. Trim the batting and lining/pocket even with the edges of the exterior cover, as needed.

5 Cut the elastic hair tie to 3" long. Center the elastic on the back of the exterior cover, with the ends extending about ¼" beyond the edge. Pin in place.

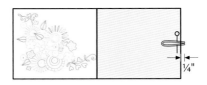

6 Use the aqua 2½"-wide strip to make binding, and then attach the binding to the needle book. Sew over the elastic as you attach the binding, backstitching a few times over the elastic to make sure it is securely attached. Hand stitch the binding to the lining side.

7 Using a rotary cutter and pinking blade, trim the edges of the cream floral rectangle. Use the FriXion pen to draw a line around the perimeter of the rectangle, about ¼" from the outer edge. Place the cream floral rectangle on the right end of the cream wool felt rectangle, about ¼" from the top, bottom, and right edges.

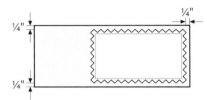

8 Using any color of floss, stitch on the marked lines using fly stitches, feather stitches, cross-stitches, and running stitches to attach the fabric to the wool page. The stitches will show on the back; make sure to hide the knots and tails between the fabric and wool layers.

9 Press to remove the marks from the FriXion pen. Press the wool page in half to make a 4" × 4⅞" rectangle. Fold the needle book in half crosswise and pin-mark the centerline. Open the needle book, lining side facing up. Place the folded wool pages on the lining, about 1/16" to the right of the centerline, with the embroidery facing up.

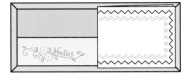

10 Open the wool page and pin in place. Machine stitch the wool page, ⅛" to the right of the fold line, backstitching at the beginning and end.

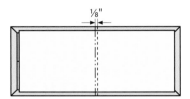

11 Center and sew one button on the embroidery end of the exterior cover. Sew the second button on the lining side, using the interior button to hide the stitches and knots of the front button.

Pocket pattern

Cover pattern

Lovebird Pincushion

Everybody needs a cute little bird to perch nearby and help with stitching, right? I designed this special project for a class I taught in beautiful Spokane, Washington. The lovely ladies at The Quilting Bee supplied the darling little molds, and all I had to do was come up with something cute to put inside! Whenever I see this pincushion I think of the laughter and conversation we enjoyed that weekend. If you don't have a metal mold, substitute a teacup or jelly jar!

FINISHED SIZE: APPROXIMATELY 4" TALL AND 3" DIAMETER

Made by Meg Hawkey

Materials

Check your supplies to see what you already have and what's needed.

Fabric and Supplies

7½" × 7½" square of floral linen for pincushion

2" × 2" square of cream floral for wings*

3" × 3" square of white wool felt for flower and leaves

3" × 4" rectangle of white linen for bird's body

6" to 8" length of beige ½"-wide seam binding (I use Hug Snug) for base of bird

Cream sewing thread

Embroidery needle, size 7

Metal mold, about 3"-diameter opening

Crushed walnut shells

You may need a bigger square if you want to position a floral motif in the center of each wing.

Polyester fiberfill stuffing

Mother-of-pearl button, ⅜" to ½" diameter, for flower center

2" length of scalloped lace for base of bird (optional)

Spanish moss for nest

Sharp toothpick for bird's beak

Orange or yellow acrylic paint or permanent pen for bird's beak

Freezer paper

Pinking shears

Hot glue gun and glue

Colored Pencils

Colors listed below are Prismacolor Premier Soft Core colored pencils.

Green to coordinate with pincushion fabric for leaves

Color to coordinate with pincushion fabric for flower

Blush Pink, PC928

Embroidery Floss

Colors listed below are for Cosmo Solid and Cosmo Seasons variegated 6-strand embroidery floss. Consult the floss photos on page 12 when using other brands.

Charcoal (895) for bird's eye

Taupe (8039) for button and flower

Preparing the Seam Binding and Beak

1 Wet the seam binding with water and accordion pleat it. Don't make the pleats too perfect, as the seam binding needs to look messy. Let the pleated binding dry on a paper towel overnight. If still damp, gently open the seam binding and allow it to fully dry.

2 Water down the acrylic paint. Either apply paint to the toothpick with a brush or simply dip one end of the toothpick in the paint. You can use a permanent marking pen instead of acrylic paint if you prefer. Let dry completely and cut the toothpick to the length you'd like for the bird's beak.

Making the Bird and Flower

1 Using the patterns on page 39, trace the shapes onto the dull side of the freezer paper the number of times indicated.

2 Press the shiny side of the freezer-paper circle onto the right side of the floral linen. Cut out one circle. Press the shiny side of the wing freezer-paper templates onto the right side of the cream floral. Cut out two wings.

3 Cut out the flower and leaf freezer-paper templates on the traced line. Using the colored pencil chosen for the flower, trace one large flower and one small flower onto the white wool felt square. Color the flower shapes. Use the green colored pencil selected for the leaves to trace two leaves onto the white wool felt square. Color the leaves. Cut out the flowers and leaves.

4 Fold the white linen rectangle in half, *right* sides out, to make a 2" × 3" rectangle. Press the shiny side of the bird freezer-paper template on one side of the folded linen rectangle. Trace around the bird template.

5 Thread a needle with a double strand of cream sewing thread and knot the ends. Sew a short running stitch around the perimeter of the bird,

leaving the bottom edge open. Knot off securely. Use the pinking shears to cut around the stitched edges of the bird.

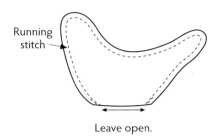

Running stitch

Leave open.

6 Stuff the bird body lightly with fiberfill. Sew across the bottom edge. This edge won't show once the bird is glued in place.

7 Use a double strand of cream thread and a small running stitch to sew a wing onto each side of the bird body.

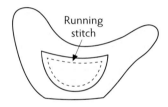

Running stitch

8 To make the eyes, thread the embroidery needle with two strands of charcoal floss and knot one end. Insert the needle into the bottom edge of the bird and come out at the spot where you want to make the eye. Make one French knot, and then insert the needle into the bird's head and bring it out where you want to make the other eye. Make one French knot, and then insert the needle into the bird's head and bring it out at the bottom edge of the bird and secure it with a knot.

9 Use the Blush Pink colored pencil to blush the bird's cheeks.

10 Layer the small flower on top of the large flower. Place the button on top. Use three strands of taupe floss to sew the button and flowers together.

Making the Pincushion

1. Cut a 2' length of three-strand taupe floss, thread the needle, and make a big knot in one end. Sew a small running stitch around the perimeter of the circle, about ¼" from the outer edge. Overlap the beginning by a stitch or two. Do not remove the needle.

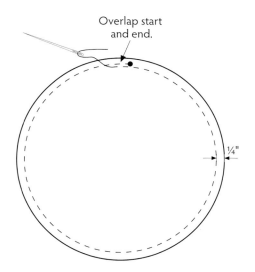

Overlap start and end.

¼"

2. Pull the thread to gather the edges of the circle, and then stuff firmly with fiberfill. Pull the thread tight and knot the thread securely.

3. Fill the metal mold about ⅔ full with crushed walnut shells. Place the stuffed circle in the mold's opening to audition the pincushion. Add more crushed walnuts if needed to help the pincushion sit a little higher; once it's glued in place, you won't be able to make any changes.

4. When you are pleased with the placement, apply a thick bead line of hot glue around the inside of the mold. Immediately place the pincushion into the mold and carefully press to secure. The metal will be hot, so be careful! Hold the pincushion in place until the glue is fully set and cool. This will take a few minutes, but it's *very important* to keep pressure on the pincushion until it has set and cooled.

5. Place a tiny dot of hot glue on the end of the painted toothpick. Insert the toothpick between the seam allowances for the bird's beak.

6. Place hot glue on the back third or so of the pincushion top. Press the Spanish moss into the glue. Then place the bird on top, adding more glue if needed. Glue the leaves and then the flower in front of the bird.

7. Sew the ends of the lace together. Glue the pleated seam binding and the lace to the pincushion at the base of the bird. Add pretty pins as desired.

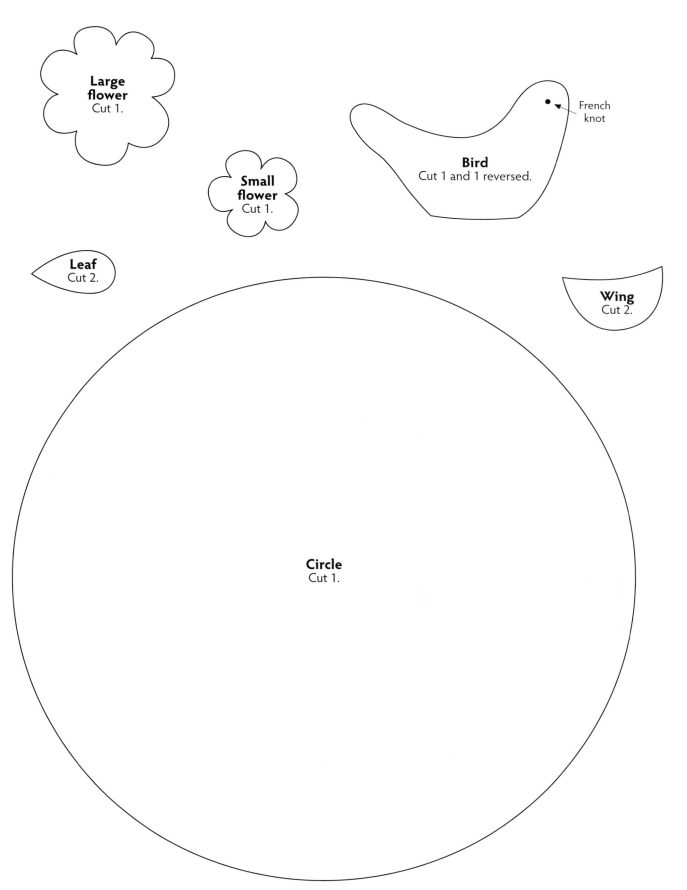

Large flower
Cut 1.

Small flower
Cut 1.

Bird
Cut 1 and 1 reversed.

French knot

Leaf
Cut 2.

Wing
Cut 2.

Circle
Cut 1.

Strawberry Basket Quilt

*S*avor the sweet fruits of strawberry season any time of year with this delectable embroidered quilt. Paired with a pieced block, this dual-sided quilt brings a double dose of stitching fun!

FINISHED QUILT: 12½" × 24½" • **FINISHED BLOCKS: 9" × 9"**

Embroidered & pieced by Meg Hawkey; quilted by Joanie Jensen

Materials

Yardage is based on 42"-wide fabric. Check your supplies to see what you already have and what's needed.

Fabric and Supplies

⅛ yard *each* of white floral and green floral for Counterchange Cross block

¼ yard of taupe floral for border

¼ yard of pink floral for binding

15" × 15" square of cream print for embroidery background

15" × 15" square of white muslin for embroidery backing

½ yard of fabric for quilt backing

17" × 29" piece of batting

Color fixative

Embroidery needle, size 7 or 8

Milliner's needle, size 3

5" spring-tension embroidery hoop

9½" × 9½" square of freezer paper

Ackfeld wire hanger (optional)

Colored Pencils

Colors listed below are Prismacolor Premier Soft Core colored pencils.

Eggshell, PC140

Sunburst Yellow, PC917

Limepeel, PC1005

French Grey (50%), PC1072

French Grey (70%), PC1074

Beige Sienna, PC1080

Kelly Green, PC1096

Embroidery Floss

Colors listed below are for Cosmo Seasons variegated 6-strand embroidery floss. Consult the floss photos on page 12 when using other brands.

Rose (5004) for strawberries

Moss (5014) for strawberry tops, leaves, and stems

Sand (5028) for basket

Pale Pink (8004) for bullion flowers and scallop trim

Ruby (8008) for trim

Fern (8016) for fly-stitched leaves

Light Yellow (8031) for flower centers

Punch (8061) for flowers

Cutting

From the white floral, cut:
2 squares, 3½" × 3½"
4 rectangles, 2" × 3½"
2 squares, 2" × 2"

From the green floral, cut:
2 squares, 3½" × 3½"
4 rectangles, 2" × 3½"
2 squares, 2" × 2"

From the taupe floral, cut:
1 strip, 3½" × 12½"
2 strips, 2" × 12½"
4 strips, 2" × 9½"

From the pink floral, cut:
3 strips, 2½" × 42"

Tracing and Tinting the Design

Refer to "General Instructions" on page 6 for in-depth information on tracing, tinting, and embroidering the design.

1 Center and trace the pattern on page 45 onto the right side of the cream square.

2 Using the colored pencils, color the design in the following order, referring to the photo above and the one on page 40 as needed.

- **Eggshell:** Shade the scalloped doily and blend.
- **Beige Sienna:** Shade the basket. Add further shading to the basket with French Grey (50%) and blend.
- **French Grey (70%):** Shade the little openings between the ribs of the basket and beneath the scallops; blend.
- **Limepeel:** Tint the leaves. Shade them with Kelly Green; blend.
- **Sunburst Yellow:** Tint the center of each daisy and blend.

3 Apply fixative to the colored design, then dry and heat set. Baste the muslin square to the wrong side of the embroidered cream square.

Embroidering the Design

Use three strands of floss and the embroidery needle to stitch the design unless otherwise indicated.

- **Moss:** Backstitch the tendrils and outline the large leaves. Fill the strawberry tops with backstitches.
- **Ruby:** Backstitch the top of the basket trim. Use pale pink floss and a blanket stitch to fill the scallops, starting on the top line. Fill the circles using a blanket stitch. Stitch two-wrap French knots along the top and bottom edges.
- **Rose:** Use a long-and-short stitch to fill in the strawberries.
- **Sand:** Backstitch the basket and handle.
- **Fern:** Fly stitch to fill the leaves.

- **Light Yellow:** Starting in the center, make outward-facing blanket stitches around the center circle. Stitch closely spaced two-wrap French knots inside the center circle. Work a tiny chain stitch around the outer circle. Stitch two-wrap French knots on the strawberries for seeds.
- **Punch:** Make double lazy daisy petals.
- **Pale Pink:** Use a milliner's needle to make 16-wrap bullion stitch petals from dot to dot.
- **Light Yellow:** Fully fill each flower center with three-wrap French knots.

Making the Counterchange Cross Block

Use ¼" seam allowances. Press the seam allowances as indicated by the arrows.

1 Join a white rectangle and a green rectangle to make a rail unit measuring 3½" square, including seam allowances. Make four units.

Make 4 units,
3½" × 3½".

2 Lay out the two white and two green 2" squares in two rows of two squares each. Sew the squares into rows. Join the rows to make a four-patch unit measuring 3½" square, including seam allowances.

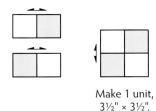

Make 1 unit,
3½" × 3½".

3 Lay out the rail units, four-patch unit, two white 3½" squares, and two green 3½" squares in three rows of three, noting the orientation of the units. Sew the pieces into rows. Join the rows to make a block measuring 9½" square, including seam allowances.

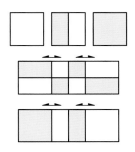

Counterchange Cross block.
Make 1 block,
9½" × 9½".

the orientation of the blocks. Sew taupe 2" × 12½" strips to opposite ends of the quilt. The quilt top should measure 12½" × 24½".

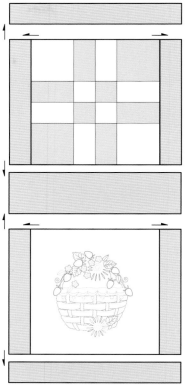

Quilt assembly

Assembling the Quilt Top

1 Refer to "Pressing the Finished Embroidery" on page 16 to press the embroidered square.

2 Refer to "Trimming the Finished Piece" on page 16 to mark lines 1" in from all four edges of the freezer-paper square. Then mark lines 1½" in from all four edges. The marked lines will help you center and arrange your design. Trim the embroidery to 9½" square and remove the freezer-paper template.

3 Sew taupe 2" × 9½" strips to the sides of the embroidery and Counterchange Cross block as shown in the quilt assembly diagram. Sew the taupe 3½" × 12½" strip between the blocks, noting

Finishing the Quilt

For help with any of the following steps, go to ShopMartingale.com/HowtoQuilt for free illustrated instructions.

1 Layer the quilt top with batting and backing. Baste the layers together.

2 Hand or machine quilt as desired. The quilt shown is machine quilted with a feather wreath in the Counterchange Cross block. The embroidered block is quilted with continuous loops in the background; the embroidered area is left unquilted. Loops are also quilted between the blocks, and feathers are quilted throughout the border.

3 Use the pink 2½"-wide strips to make binding, and then attach the binding to the quilt.

Strawberry Basket Quilt

Honeybee Snap Bag

You can use my little embroidery design or a piece of vintage embroidery to make a sweet snap bag. The purse frame kits are available in quilt shops and craft stores. I've made almost 300 of the bags for various stitching retreats; the project is so simple, you'll be amazed!

FINISHED SIZE: APPROXIMATELY 6½" × 6½"

Made by Meg Hawkey

Materials

Check your supplies to see what you already have and what's needed.

Fabric and Supplies

10" × 11" rectangle of white linen for bag front embroidery

10" × 11" rectangle of white muslin for embroidery backing

8" × 9" rectangle of green dot for bag back

8" × 18" strip of green check for bag lining

Brown Pigma Pen, size 01

Color fixative

Embroidery needle, size 7

5" spring-tension embroidery hoop

Jelly Clip purse frame, 14 cm

Aleene's Tacky glue

Wooden skewers

Colored Pencils

Colors listed below are Prismacolor Premier Soft Core colored pencils.

Aquamarine, PC905

Sunburst Yellow, PC917

Pink, PC929

Black, PC935

Chartreuse, PC989

Light Aqua, PC992

Limepeel, PC1005

Beige Sienna, PC1080

Kelly Green, PC1096

Moss Green, PC1097

Embroidery Floss

Colors listed below are for Cosmo Solid and Cosmo Seasons variegated 6-strand embroidery floss. Consult the floss photos on page 12 when using other brands.

Honey (701) for bee body and flower centers

Charcoal (895) for bee body and eye

White (8001) for lily of the valley flowers

Ruby (8008) for bleeding heart tops

Olive (8015) for hydrangea flowers

Green (8021) for leaves and stems

Pine (8024) for leaves and stems

Khaki (8040) for bleeding heart bottoms, lily of the valley flowers, and bee wings

Blue (8054) for jar

Tracing and Tinting the Design

Refer to "General Instructions" on page 6 for more in-depth information on tracing, tinting, and embroidering the design.

1 Center and trace the pattern on page 50 onto the right side of the white linen rectangle using the brown Pigma pen.

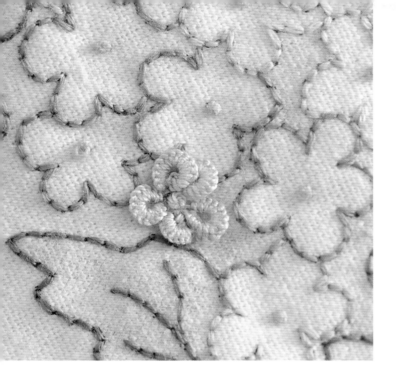

3 Apply fixative to the colored design, then dry and heat set. Baste the muslin rectangle to the wrong side of the white linen rectangle.

Embroidering the Design

Use two strands of floss and the embroidery needle to stitch the design unless otherwise indicated.

- **Ruby:** Backstitch the bleeding heart tops and buds.
- **Blue:** Backstitch the jar.
- **Honey:** Fill the yellow "stripes" on the bee's body with cross-stitches.
- **Charcoal:** Backstitch the bee's body and make a one-wrap French knot for the eye. Use one strand to backstitch the legs.
- **Green:** Backstitch the hydrangea leaves and the lily of the valley stems in the lower-right corner.
- **White:** Fill the lily of the valley flowers with columns of cross-stitches, making sure to fill the area fully.
- **Khaki:** Using the medium to light area of the floss, backstitch the bleeding heart bottoms. Use one strand to backstitch the lily of the valley flowers and the bee's wings.
- **Pine:** Backstitch the lily of the valley leaves and remaining stems.
- **Olive:** Backstitch the hydrangea flowers. Use four strands to make three 15-knot cast-on flowers with five petals each.
- **Honey:** Make a three-wrap French knot in the center of each hydrangea flower and a four-wrap French knot in the center of each cast-on flower.

2 Using the colored pencils, color the design in the following order, referring to the photo on page 49 as needed.

- **Light Aqua:** Lightly tint the jar. Shade with Aquamarine. Blend.
- **Limepeel:** Lightly tint the lily of the valley leaves. Shade them with Kelly Green; blend. *Do not* tint the lily of the valley flowers.
- **Limepeel:** Tint the hydrangea leaves. Shade them with Kelly Green and Moss Green; blend.
- **Pink:** Tint the tops of the bleeding hearts. Shade them darker with Pink; blend.
- **Chartreuse:** Lightly shade the bleeding heart bottoms on one side; blend.
- **Limepeel:** Very lightly tint to create a hazy background in the bouquet behind the hydrangea. Shade with Kelly Green and Moss Green; blend.
- **Chartreuse:** Tint the hydrangea flowers, leaving many of the petals untinted; blend.
- **Beige Sienna:** Shade the bee's wings very lightly and blend.
- **Sunburst Yellow and Black:** Tint the bee's body. Blend the stripes separately.

Assembling the Bag

1 Using the bag pattern on page 51, center and trace the bag outline on the wrong side of the embroidered bag front. Mark the top center of the bag. Also mark the dart placement at the bottom corners. Repeat to trace the bag outline and mark the darts on the green dot rectangle for the bag back. Then trace the bag outline twice on the green check rectangle and mark the darts to make two lining pieces. Cut out the embroidered bag front, bag back, and two lining pieces.

2 On the bag front, align the marked lines for the darts, right sides together. Sew the darts. Repeat to sew the darts on the bag back and both lining pieces.

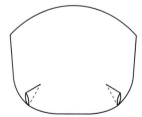

4 Place the lining inside the outer bag, right sides together. Pin around the top edge. Sew around the top edge, leaving a 2" opening for turning.

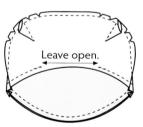

Leave open.

3 Layer the bag front and back, right sides together, and sew around the bottom, curved edges. Clip the curves. Repeat to sew the lining pieces together.

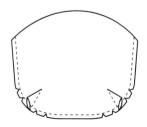

5 Turn the bag right side out through the opening, and tuck the lining into the outer bag. Topstitch about ⅛" from the top of the bag to close the opening.

Bag-Making Tips

You can use a cotton swab and water to remove mistakes with the tacky glue, even on the fabric, as long as you do it right away! Do not use hot glue, which will solidify too quickly.

I don't recommend putting anything super heavy in these bags, because the fabric may pull out of the frame. This has never happened to me, but I always feel like it could.

6 Place a bead of tacky glue into the channels of the front and back of the purse frame. Use a wooden skewer to carefully poke the topstitched edge into the channel, starting on the sides and working toward the center. You'll have to gently gather the fabric around the top of the bag.

7 Until the glue is dry, hold the bag by supporting the fabric and plastic top at the same time. Then allow the bag to dry overnight or longer.

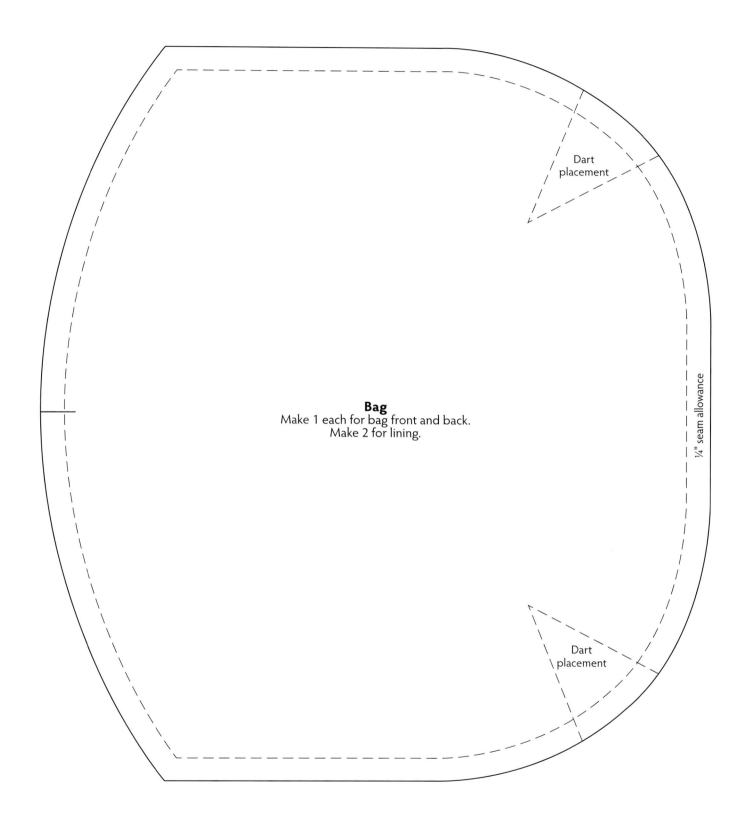

Bag
Make 1 each for bag front and back.
Make 2 for lining.

Dart placement

Dart placement

¼" seam allowance

Heartfelt Blossom Pendants

I love to find ways to "wear my heart on my sleeve"—that is, to use my embroidery on clothing or jewelry for the whole world to see! These pendants can function as necklaces, bracelets, scissor fobs, or zipper pulls for a project bag or purse. And who doesn't love playing with beads and charms? The sky's the limit!

FINISHED SIZE: 1¼" DIAMETER

Made by Meg Hawkey

Materials

Materials are sufficient to make all 3 pendants. Check your supplies to see what you already have and what's needed.

Fabric and Supplies

3 squares, 7" × 7" *each*, of light print for embroidery background*

3 squares, 2" × 2" *each*, of batting

Brown Pigma pen, size 01

Color fixative

Embroidery needle, size 7 or 8

Milliner's needle, size 3

5" spring-tension embroidery hoop

Sewing thread

E6000 glue

Cotton swabs

Small binding clips

*I used a beige polka dot for 2 of the pendants and a white floral for the third. If you would like to use 1 fabric for all 3 pendants, you'll need a 7" × 20" rectangle. Trace all 3 embroidery patterns onto the rectangle, leaving about 4" between the designs.

Jewelry Materials

3 silver circle pendants kits, 32 mm

2 eye pins, 3" (21 gauge)

1 pin with large head

2 lobster claw clasps, 22 mm

4 split rings, 6 mm or 7 mm

3 or 4 crimp beads, round, smooth size 1

9 beads in size and color of your choice

1 heart charm

5 bead caps

Ball chain with clasp for necklace

Beadalon 0.015 beading wire (7 strand)

Round-tip pliers

Needle-nose pliers

Split-ring pliers

Circle Pendant

I used Embroidery Kit Grande Circle Pendants by Nunn Design. The large jump rings are already attached, so no additional jewelry-making tools are required. You can find circle pendants online at NunnDesign.com.

Colored Pencils

Colors listed below are Prismacolor Premier Soft Core colored pencils.

Permanent Red, PC122

Sunburst Yellow, PC917

Pink, PC929

Limepeel, PC1005

Tracing and Embroidering the Designs

Refer to "General Instructions" on page 6 for in-depth information on tracing, tinting, and embroidering the designs. Embroidery patterns are on page 56. Use three strands of floss and the embroidery needle to stitch the designs unless otherwise indicated.

Rose Pendant

1 Center and trace the rose pattern onto the right side of a light square using the brown Pigma pen. Be sure to trace the outer circle.

2 Using the colored pencils, color the design in the following order, referring to the photo at left as needed.

- **Limepeel:** Tint the background of the leaves; blend.
- **Sunburst Yellow:** Tint the yellow flower-center area; blend.
- **Pink:** Shade the petals; blend.
- **Permanent Red:** Shade around the outer edges of the petals; blend.

3 Apply fixative to the colored design. Let dry and then heat set.

4 Use Rose floss to backstitch the flower petal outlines.

5 Use Moss floss to fill the leaves with fly stitches.

6 Use Light Yellow floss to make two-wrap French knots in the flower center and one-wrap French knot dots in the background.

Embroidery Floss

Colors listed below are for Cosmo Seasons variegated 6-strand embroidery floss. Consult the floss photos on page 12 when using other brands.

Rose (5004) for flower and heart

Red (5005) for bullion flower

Bright Yellow (5009) for flower center

Moss (5014) for leaves

Aqua (5016) for dots on bullion petals

Light Yellow (8031) for flower centers, background dots, and bullion petals

Bullion Flower

1 Center and trace the bullion flower pattern onto the right side of a light square using the brown Pigma pen. Be sure to trace the outer circle.

2 Using the colored pencils, color the design in the following order, referring to the photo as needed.

✦ **Limepeel:** Tint the background of the leaves; blend.

✦ **Sunburst Yellow:** Tint the yellow flower-center area; blend.

3 Apply fixative to the colored design. Let dry and then heat set.

4 Use Moss floss to fill the leaves with fly stitches.

5 Use Red floss and the milliner's needle to make 16-wrap bullion petals, stitching from dot to dot.

6 Use Bright Yellow floss to make one-wrap French knots in the flower center.

Modern Heart

1 Center and trace the modern heart pattern onto the right side of a light square using the brown Pigma pen. Be sure to trace the outer circle.

2 Using the colored pencils, color the design in the following order, referring to the photo as needed.

✦ **Limepeel:** Tint the background of the leaves; blend.

✦ **Pink:** Tint the heart. Shade the heart with Permanent Red; blend.

3 Apply fixative to the colored design. Let dry and then heat set.

4 Use two strands of Rose floss to outline the heart with a tiny chain stitch.

5 Use two strands of Moss floss to make tiny double lazy daisy stitches for leaves.

6 Use the milliner's needle and the Light Yellow floss to make five 16-wrap bullion stitches. To curve the two outer bullions, couch them in place with one strand of floss.

7 Use Aqua floss to make three-wrap French knots.

Assembling the Pendants

1 Press each finished embroidery well. Trim the embroidery around the traced circle.

2 Cut each batting square into a circle using the metal disk in the pendant kit as a template.

3 Cut a piece of sewing thread approximately 48" long and double it. Thread a sewing needle with the doubled thread and then pull the ends together to make four strands. Make a big, strong knot in the end of the threads.

4 Sew scant ¼"-long running stitches around the edge of each circle until you reach the starting point again. Take an extra stitch that overlaps the starting point but is closer to the edge of the fabric so as not to accidentally sew through the thread already in the fabric.

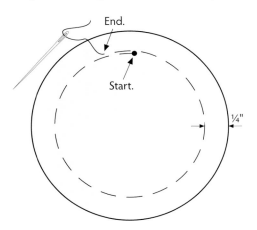

5 For each pendant, place a batting circle and then the flat metal disk on the wrong side of an embroidered circle. Pull the threads to gather and tightly encase them—the tighter the better to make the edges smooth.

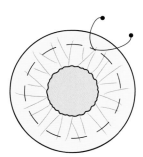

6 Knot off the thread securely and trim the ends of the thread to about ¼" long.

7 Place the gathered disk into the bezel to audition it.

8 Make a little pool of glue in the center of the bezel. Use a cotton swab to carefully spread the glue around, getting it very near the edges of the bezel. The pool should be thicker at the center, where all of the gathers are concentrated. If it's too thick near the edge, it will squeeze out when the embroidery is placed inside.

9 Place the embroidery in the bezel. Use four or five little binding clips to hold the embroidery firmly in the bezel. Let dry overnight. You can handle the pendant to add a chain or beading, but allow the glue to cure for a few days before actually using or wearing the pendant. It's easiest to just add a ball chain or cording, but there are many great tutorials online that will walk you through simple beading and finishing techniques.

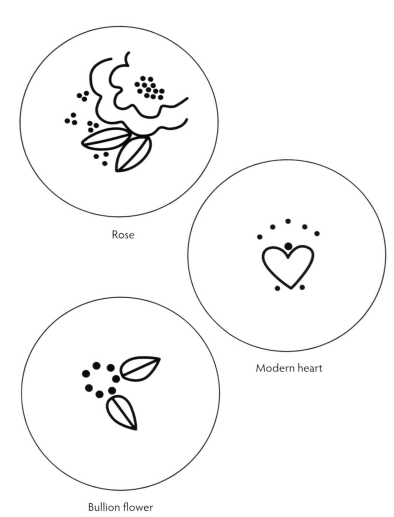

Rose

Modern heart

Bullion flower

Heartfelt Blossom Pendants

Needlework Garden Stitch Sampler

*F*ifteen little inchies! I love how coloring the backgrounds gives the squares the appearance of appliquéd fabric. Polka dots, checks, and even plaid! How fun is that? There are a lot of different stitches packed into this small embroidery and you'll have a real sense of accomplishment when you've completed them all.

FINISHED SIZE: 8" × 10" (without frame)

Made by Meg Hawkey

Materials

Check your supplies to see what you already have and what's needed.

Fabric and Supplies

15" × 20" rectangle of vanilla linen for embroidery background

15" × 20" rectangle of white muslin for embroidery backing

5" spring-tension embroidery hoop

Embroidery needle, size 7 or 8

Milliner's needle, size 3

Brown Pigma pen, size 01

Light box

Color fixative

Framing Materials

To frame your design like the project shown, you will need the following (see "Framing Your Embroideries" on page 17).

Frame with 8" × 10" opening

8" × 10" piece of foam core

8" × 10" piece of batting

Pins with large heads

Heavy thread, such as crochet thread, or 6 strands of embroidery floss

Milliner's needle, size 1, or chenille needle

Strips of fabric to enlarge your embroidery (optional)

Colored Pencils

Colors listed below are Prismacolor Premier Soft Core colored pencils.

Blush Pink, PC928

Limepeel, PC1005

Deco Yellow, PC1011

French Grey (70%), PC1074

Beige Sienna, PC1080

Embroidery Floss

Colors listed below are for Cosmo Seasons variegated 6-strand embroidery floss. Consult the floss photos on page 12 when using other brands.

Moss (5014) for leaves, vines, stems, bud caps, and square outline

Pink (8006) for flower petals, heart, floss card, strawberry, stripes, and square outline

Light Yellow (8031) for flower centers, circle flowers, bee wings, and square outline

Taupe (8039) for letters, floss card, bee body and legs, flowers, stem, and square outline

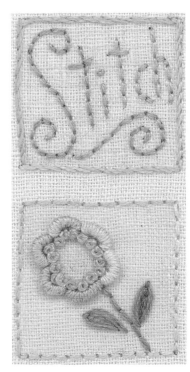

Tracing and Tinting the Design

Refer to "General Instructions" on page 6 for in-depth information on tracing, tinting, and embroidering the design.

1 Using a light box and the brown Pigma pen, center and trace the pattern on page 61 onto the right side of the vanilla linen rectangle.

2 Using the colored pencils and starting with square 1 in the upper-left corner, color the design in the following order, referring to the photo on page 60 as needed. The instructions below correspond to the squares in each row and are numbered from left to right and from the top row to the bottom row.

- **Square 1**: Lightly shade the background area with Beige Sienna. Tint the leaves with Limepeel. Shade the flower with Blush Pink. Shade the flower center with Deco Yellow. Blend the colors separately.

- **Square 2**: Sharpen the Beige Sienna and Blush Pink pencils. Draw a grid with the Blush Pink pencil. Draw another grid with the Beige Sienna pencil about ⅛" from the pink grid to make a plaid pattern. *Do not blend.*

- **Square 3**: Sharpen the Blush Pink pencil. Draw vertical stripes on the background of the square. *Do not blend.*

- **Square 4**: Sharpen the Blush Pink pencil and then make large polka dots on the background of the square. *Do not blend.* Tint the bud cap with Limepeel; blend.

- **Square 5**: Use Beige Sienna to very lightly shade white stripes. Use Blush Pink to very lightly shade pink stripes. Blend each separately.

- **Square 6**: Sharpen the Blush Pink pencil and draw vertical and horizontal lines on the square to make a grid. *Do not blend.*

- **Square 7**: Sharpen the Limepeel pencil and then make large polka dots on the background of the square. *Do not blend.*

- **Square 8**: Sharpen the Blush Pink pencil and then make a large gridwork check pattern on the bottom part of the square. *Do not blend.*

- **Square 9**: Shade the top and bottom areas of the floss card with Beige Sienna; blend. Tint and shade the center portion of the card with Blush Pink; blend.

- **Square 10**: Sharpen the Blush Pink pencil and draw randomly placed little circles on the square. Tint everything that lies *outside* the little circles. Blend the pink area carefully so that you don't pull the pink into the white dots.

- **Square 11**: Tint the center of the ring of dots with Deco Yellow; blend. Tint and shade the background of the square with Blush Pink; blend.

- **Square 12**: Tint the leaf and bud cap with Limepeel; blend. Tint the center of the flower with Deco Yellow. Tint and shade the flowers petals with Blush Pink; blend. Shade the bee's wings with a tiny bit of Beige Sienna; blend. Tint the bee's yellow stripes with Deco Yellow and the dark stripes with French Grey.

- **Square 13**: Sharpen the Blush Pink pencil and make small dots on the background of the square. *Do not blend.*

- **Square 14**: Very lightly shade the flowers with Blush Pink; blend.

- **Square 15**: Tint the flower center with Deco Yellow. Blend. Sharpen the Beige Sienna and Blush Pink pencils. Draw a plaid background in the same way you did for square 2. *Do not blend.*

3 Apply fixative to the colored design. Let dry and then heat set. Baste the muslin rectangle to the wrong side of the linen rectangle. For best results, baste a grid between the squares.

Embroidering the Design

Use two strands of floss and the embroidery needle to stitch the designs unless otherwise indicated.

- **For square 1:** Using the Pink floss, backstitch the flower. Use Moss floss to backstitch the vine and leaves. Use the darkest area of the Light Yellow floss to backstitch the flower center and outline the square.

For square 2: Use Moss floss to backstitch the stem and make double lazy daisy leaves. Use Pink floss to make a satin stitch–filled heart and to backstitch the square's outline.

For square 3: Use Taupe floss and a tiny chain stitch to outline the square. Use Moss floss to make double lazy daisy leaves. Use Pink floss to make three two-wrap French knot dots. Use three strands of Pink floss and the milliner's needle to make five 16-knot cast-on stitch petals. Use Light Yellow floss to make a three-wrap French knot for the flower center.

For square 4: Use Moss floss to backstitch the stem and bud cap and to make double lazy daisy leaves. Use Pink floss to make two-wrap pistil stitches for the flower petals. Use Light Yellow floss and a backstitch to outline the square.

For square 5: Use Pink floss and a backstitch to outline the square. Use Pink floss and a tiny chain stitch to make the stripes.

For square 6: Use Taupe floss and a backstitch to make the word *Stitch* and the swirl, and to make a one-wrap French knot for the dot in *Stitch*. Use Pink floss and a stem stitch to outline the square. When stitching the outline, knot the thread at each corner

of the square and stitch each side separately. Don't try to stitch around the corners, because the stitch will roll in.

For square 7: Use Moss floss to fly stitch the left stem. Use Taupe floss to fly stitch the right stem and make two-wrap French knots on the left stem. Use Taupe floss and a backstitch to outline the square. Use Light Yellow floss to make two-wrap French knots on the right stem.

For square 8: Use Light Yellow floss and a tiny chain stitch to make a horizontal line across the square. Use Moss floss and a backstitch to outline the square. Use three strands of Pink floss and the milliner's needle to make four 18-wrap bullion stitches from dot to dot.

For square 9: Use Taupe floss and a backstitch to stitch the top and bottom areas of the floss card. Use Pink floss and a backstitch to stitch the thread on the card.

For square 10: Use Pink floss to blanket-stitch around the square. When you reach a corner, make a stitch that goes diagonally in the corner, then make a knot on the back or take a tiny stitch on the back to anchor the stitch. Continue stitching along the next side of the square.

For square 11: Use Moss floss to backstitch the stem and to make double lazy daisy leaves. Use three strands of Pink floss and the size 3 milliner's needle to make six 18-wrap bullion stitches from dot to dot around the flower. Use Light Yellow floss to make three-wrap French knots in a ring inside the petals. Use Pink floss and a backstitch to outline the square.

For square 12: Use Moss floss to backstitch the stem and bud cap, fly stitch inside the leaf, and backstitch around the outer edge of the leaf. Use Pink floss to backstitch the flower petals. Use Light Yellow floss and a backstitch to outline the bee's wings and to make two-wrap French knots for the flower center. Use one strand of Light Yellow floss to make little fly stitches in the bee's right wing. Use Taupe floss to backstitch the bee's body. Use one strand of Taupe floss and a straight stitch to make the bee's legs.

For square 13: Use Pink floss and a tiny chain stitch to outline the square. Use Moss floss to backstitch the stems and make double lazy daisy leaves. Use Light Yellow floss and a blanket stitch to make circle flowers. Use Taupe floss to make three-wrap French knot flower centers.

For square 14: Use Pink floss and a long-and-short stitch to fill the strawberry, working from bottom to top. Use Green floss to backstitch the vine and make single lazy daisy leaves at the top of the strawberry. Use Taupe floss to backstitch the flowers. Use Light Yellow to make three-wrap French knot flower centers and to make tiny, single lazy daisy seeds on the strawberry.

For square 15: Use Light Yellow floss to backstitch around the flower center, make three cross-stitches, and make two-wrap French knots. Use Taupe floss and a backstitch to outline the square. Use three strands of Pink floss to make double lazy daisy petals.

Framing the Embroidery

1 Place the batting on top of the foam core. Center the embroidered linen on top of the batting. Pin in place, making sure the linen is taut and smooth. Stretch the linen over the foam core/batting as described in "Framing Your Embroideries" on page 17.

2 Place the embroidery in the frame and secure it with the clips that came with the frame.

Blooming Baskets Quilt

What could be prettier than baskets surrounding block centers that are filled to the brim with embroidery? This design looks difficult, but that's the magical part! The embroidery is actually really easy, and the piecing is even easier. I embroidered all the block centers on one piece of linen. I used an assembly-line method and stitched one element at a time, then cut them apart. The embroidery only took four days!

FINISHED QUILT: 66½" × 66½" • **FINISHED BLOCKS: 16" × 16"**

Embroidered & pieced by Meg Hawkey; quilted by Joanie Jensen

Materials

Check your supplies to see what you already have and what's needed.

Fabric and Supplies

½ yard of oat linen for embroidery background

2⅓ yards of cream floral for blocks, sashing, and inner border

2⅛ yards of taupe polka dot for blocks and outer border

¼ yard *each* of 12 light prints for blocks and outer border

½ yard of pink print for blocks

1⅞ yards of pink floral for blocks, middle border, cornerstones, and binding

4⅛ yards of fabric for backing

73" × 73" piece of batting

Embroidery needle, size 7 or 8

Milliner's needle, size 3

5" spring-tension embroidery hoop

13½" × 13½" square of freezer paper

FriXion pen

Copy paper

Fine-tip permanent marker

Light box

Embroidery Floss

Colors listed below are for Cosmo Seasons variegated 6-strand embroidery floss. Consult the floss photos on page 12 when using other brands.

Flamingo (5001) for lazy daisy flower*

Rouge Pink (5002) for bullion flower

Sage (5013) for flower-center rings*

Ivory (8002) for pistil flower

Fern (8016) for vines and leaves*

Light Yellow (8031) for flower centers

Punch (8061) for flower center

*You'll need 3 skeins of Flamingo and 2 skeins each of Sage and Fern.

Cutting

All measurements include ¼" seam allowances.

From the oat linen, cut:
1 rectangle, 16" × 31"

From the *lengthwise* grain of the cream floral, cut:
2 strips, 2½" × 56½"
2 strips, 2½" × 52½"

From the remainder of the cream floral, cut:
36 squares, 4½" × 4½"
72 squares, 2⅞" × 2⅞"
12 strips, 2½" × 16½"
36 squares, 2½" × 2½"

From the taupe polka dot, cut:
8 strips, 3½" × 42"; crosscut into 84 squares, 3½" × 3½"
10 strips, 2⅞" × 42"; crosscut into 126 squares, 2⅞" × 2⅞"
5 strips, 2½" × 42"; crosscut into 72 squares, 2½" × 2½"

Continued on page 64

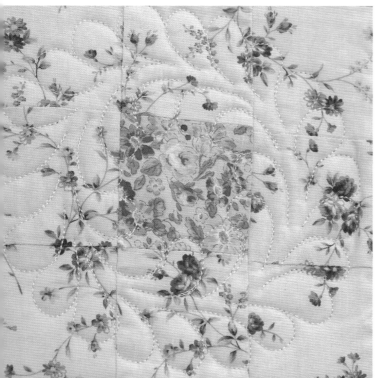

Continued from page 63

From *each* light print, cut:

4 rectangles, 3½" × 6½" (48 total; 8 are extra)

5 squares, 2⅞" × 2⅞" (60 total; 6 are extra)

From the pink print, cut:

5 strips, 2½" × 42"; crosscut into 36 rectangles, 2½" × 4½"

From the *lengthwise* grain of the pink floral, cut:

2 strips, 2½" × 60½"

2 strips, 2½" × 56½"

5 strips, 2½" × 58"

40 squares, 2½" × 2½"

Tracing the Design

Refer to "General Instructions" on page 6 for in-depth information on tracing and embroidering the block centers.

1 Measuring 3" in from the edges and using a FriXion pen, draw a grid of nine 5" squares on the linen rectangle. Using a larger rectangle will allow you to comfortably hoop and stitch the squares without wasting too much fabric.

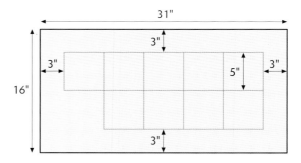

2 Trace the pattern on page 69 onto paper using a fine-tip permanent marker so that you will be able to easily see the marks through the linen.

3 Place the traced pattern on your light box. Center and trace the embroidery pattern, using a FriXion pen, within each of the 5" squares. The design *must* be centered because the squares will be trimmed to 4½" × 4½" after they're embroidered.

Embroidering the Block Centers

It will be faster and easier if you embroider the flat elements first. I recommend working the stitches in the order listed to minimize having the hoop and floss catch on the dimensional petals. With dark linen, there is no need to back the embroidery with muslin. Use three strands of floss and the embroidery needle to stitch the design throughout.

- **Fern:** Backstitch the vines and make double lazy daisy stitches for the small leaves.
- **Sage:** Make tiny chain-stitched flower-center rings.
- **Light Yellow:** Backstitch the cross-hatching. Make a buttonhole-stitched circle center for the daisy.
- **Punch:** Make a buttonhole-stitched circle center for the pistil stitch flower.
- **Fern:** Make large leaves filled with fly stitches.

- **Ivory:** Make two-wrap pistil stitch petals.
- **Flamingo:** Stitch triple lazy daisy petals.
- **Rouge Pink:** Use a milliner's needle to make 18-wrap bullion-stitched petals, working from dot to dot.
- **Light Yellow:** Make a ring of two-wrap French knots inside the bullion petals.

Press the embroidered squares well from the wrong side and then from the front (the marked lines will disappear). Cut a 4½" square of freezer paper. Referring to "Trimming the Finished Piece" on page 16, mark lines ⅜" in from all four edges of the freezer-paper template. The marked lines will help you center the design. Trim the embroidery to 4½" square and remove the freezer-paper template.

Making the Blocks

Use ¼" seam allowances. Press the seam allowances as indicated by the arrows.

1 Mark a diagonal line from corner to corner on the wrong side of the cream floral 2⅞" squares. Layer a marked square on a taupe 2⅞" square, right sides together. Sew ¼" from both sides of the drawn line. Cut the unit apart on the marked line to make two half-square-triangle units measuring 2½" square, including seam allowances. Make 144 units.

Make 144 units,
2½" × 2½".

2 Mark a diagonal line from corner to corner on the wrong side of the light 2⅞" squares. Repeat step 1 using the light squares and the remaining taupe 2⅞" squares to make 108 half-square-triangle units measuring 2½" square, including seam allowances.

Make 108 units,
2½" × 2½".

3 Mark a diagonal line from corner to corner on the wrong side of the taupe 2½" squares. Place a marked square on one end of a pink print 2½" × 4½" rectangle, right sides together. Sew on the marked line. Trim the excess corner fabric, ¼" from the stitched line. Place a marked square on the opposite end of the pink rectangle. Sew and trim as before to make a flying-geese unit that measures 2½" × 4½", including seam allowances. Make 36 units.

Make 36 units,
2½" × 4½".

4 Lay out four units from step 1, three units from step 2, one cream floral 2½" square, and one pink floral 2½" square in three rows of three, noting the orientation of the units. Sew the pieces into rows. Join the rows to make a corner unit measuring 6½" square, including seam allowances. Make 36 units.

 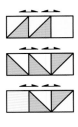

Make 36 units,
6½" × 6½".

5 Sew a flying-geese unit to a cream floral 4½" square to make a side unit measuring 4½" × 6½", including seam allowances. Make 36 units.

Make 36 units,
4½" × 6½".

6 Lay out four corner units, four side units, and one embroidered square in three rows of three, noting the orientation of the units. Sew the pieces into rows. Join the rows to make a block measuring 16½" square, including seam allowances. Make nine blocks.

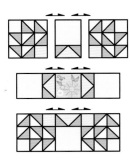 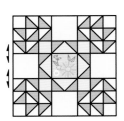

Make 9 blocks,
16½" × 16½".

Making the Outer Border

1 Mark a diagonal line from corner to corner on the wrong side of 80 of the taupe 3½" squares. Place a marked square on one end of a light 3½" × 6½" rectangle, right sides together. Sew on the marked line. Trim the excess corner fabric ¼" from the stitched line. Place a marked square on the opposite end of the light rectangle. Sew and trim as before to make a flying-geese unit that measures 3½" × 6½", including seam allowances. Make 40 units.

Make 40 units, 3½" × 6½".

2 Join 10 flying-geese units to make a side border measuring 3½" × 60½", including seam allowances. Make two. Make two more borders in the same way, and then add a taupe 3½" square to each end. The top and bottom borders should measure 3½" × 66½", including seam allowances.

Side border.
Make 2 borders, 3½" × 60½".

Top/bottom border.
Make 2 borders, 3½" × 66½".

Assembling the Quilt Top

1 Join three blocks and two cream floral 2½" × 16½" strips to make a block row measuring 16½" × 52½", including seam allowances. Make three rows.

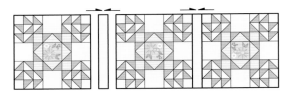

Make 3 rows, 16½" × 52½".

2 Join three cream floral 2½" × 16½" strips and two pink floral 2½" squares to make a sashing row measuring 2½" × 52½", including seam allowances. Make two rows.

Make 2 rows, 2½" × 52½".

3 Lay out the block rows and sashing rows, alternating them as shown in the quilt assembly diagram on page 69. Join the rows. The quilt-top center should measure 52½" square, including seam allowances.

4 Sew cream floral 52½"-long strips to opposite sides of the quilt top. Sew cream floral 56½"-long strips to the top and bottom of the quilt top. The quilt top should measure 56½" square, including seam allowances.

5 Sew pink floral 56½"-long strips to opposite sides of the quilt top. Sew pink floral 60½"-long strips to the top and bottom of the quilt top. The quilt top should measure 60½" square, including seam allowances.

Blooms and Blossoms

6 Sew 60½"-long outer borders to opposite sides of the quilt top. Sew 66½"-long outer borders to the top and bottom of the quilt top. The quilt top should now measure 66½" square.

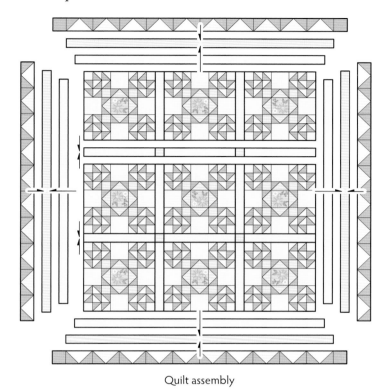

Quilt assembly

Finishing the Quilt

For help with any of the following steps, go to ShopMartingale.com/HowtoQuilt for free illustrated instructions.

1 Layer the quilt top with batting and backing. Baste the layers together.

2 Hand or machine quilt as desired. The quilt shown is machine quilted with curved lines in each block and a curved diagonal grid between the blocks. Feathers are quilted in the inner border, loops are quilted in the middle border, and swirls and straight lines are quilted in the outer border.

3 Use the pink floral 2½" × 58" strips to make binding, and then attach the binding to the quilt.

Blooming Baskets

Summer Charm Pin

Choose from the six designs to personalize your cheerful little pin. You can wear it or pin it to a bag or needlebook. Which designs? What colors? So many fun choices to make!

FINISHED SIZE: 3" LONG (without bow)

Made by Meg Hawkey

Materials

Check your supplies to see what you already have and what's needed.

Fabric and Supplies

7" × 7" square of white solid for embroidery background

7" × 7" square of white muslin for embroidery backing

Scraps of white wool felt for charm backings

Brown Pigma pen, size 01

Color fixative

Embroidery needle, size 7

Milliner's needle, size 3 (optional)

5" spring-tension embroidery hoop

11" length of double-sided ribbon for bow

3"-long kilt pin with 3 loops

White sewing thread

Prismacolor Premier Soft Core colored pencils in the colors of your choice

Coordinating colors of Cosmo embroidery floss

Tracing and Tinting the Design

Refer to "General Instructions" on page 6 for in-depth information on tracing, tinting, and embroidering the designs. Referring to the patterns on page 73, choose three designs to use for your pin.

1 Center and trace three patterns onto the right side of the white solid square, using a brown Pigma pen and leaving about ¼" between the designs. Be sure to trace the outer line on each design.

2 Using colored pencils and referring to the photo on page 72, tint the designs as desired. I lightly tinted the background on three charms, made dots on two charms, and marked a grid on one charm.

3 Apply fixative to the colored design. Let dry and then heat set. Baste the muslin square to the wrong side of the white square.

Embroidering the Design

Use two strands of any color of floss and the embroidery needle to stitch the design unless otherwise indicated.

1 On the heart-shaped charm, backstitch the flower petals and upper-left leaf. Fill the lower-left leaf with fly stitches. Stitch two-wrap French knots in the flower center and three-wrap French knots in the upper-left corner.

2 On the oval charm with the heart, chain stitch the stem. Make double lazy daisy stitches for the leaves and satin stitch the heart.

3 On the oval charm with the blue flower, backstitch the stem and satin stitch the bud cap. Make double lazy daisies for the leaves. Use three strands of floss and the milliner's needle to make five 10-wrap bullion stitches for the straight petals and one 2-wrap pistil stitch in the center.

4. On the rectangular charm, fly stitch the bottom half of the stem and backstitch the top part. Make two-wrap French knots for the top lavender blossoms and three-wrap French knots for the bottom lavender blossoms.

5. On the square charm, make double lazy daisies for the leaves. Use three strands of floss and the milliner's needle to make five 14-wrap bullion stitches for the curved petals. Stitch a ring of two-wrap French knots with a cross-stitch in the center for the flower center.

6. On the circle charm, backstitch the stems and cherries. Make double lazy daisies for the leaves.

Making the Charms

1. When the embroidery is complete, use white sewing thread to sew a tiny running stitch around the perimeter of each design, just inside the marked outer line.

2. Press, and then remove the basting threads. Cut out each charm on the line or barely inside the line.

3. Place the charms on the white wool felt, leaving about ½" between charms. Baste. Trim the wool backing even with the edges of the charms.

4. Hiding the knots and tails and working from the embroidery side, blanket-stitch around the edges of each charm, sewing through both layers. When you reach a corner, take a tiny stitch in the wool at the edge to secure the thread, or it will roll inward.

5. When you are back to where you started, knot off at the edge and hide the tail of the floss by passing it through the backing.

6. Decide where you'd like to attach each charm to the pin. Thread a needle with six strands of light-colored floss. Insert the needle and floss through the wool back of a charm. Knot the floss near, but *not on*, the top edge of the charm.

7 Insert the needle from front to back through the pin's ring. Decide on the length of the little hanging loop. Turn the charm and pin over, and insert the needle into the wool back again. Knot off and then thread the tails into the needle. Insert needle between the layers to hide thread tails.

8 Repeat steps 6 and 7 to attach all the charms. You can hang the square charm from the top or one of the corners. Hang the heart-shaped charm from one side of the top or from two loops.

9 Tie a neat bow in the ribbon and trim the ends. You may need to turn one end over so that the front of the ribbon shows. If so, sew it in place on the back of the bow.

10 Use a double strand of thread to sew the bow to the bottom of the pin in two or three places. If you sew the ribbon in only one place, it will tend to twist and turn around.

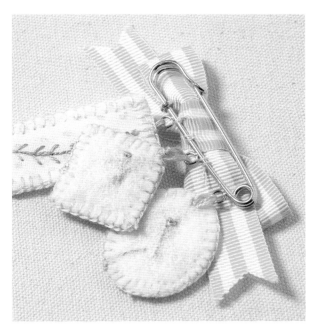

Hide the tail ends of the floss as neatly as possible between the layers of wool and fabric.

Hiding the Knots and Tails

Insert the unknotted floss through charm's back. Bring needle out between layers along charm's edge, leaving tail hidden between layers. Make a small stitch, passing needle through loop to knot and secure thread. Continue stitching. To end, again make a knot at charm's edge; insert needle between layers and out through charm's back. Gently pull on thread tail; clip it close to the fabric. It will sink between the layers.

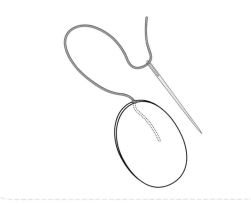

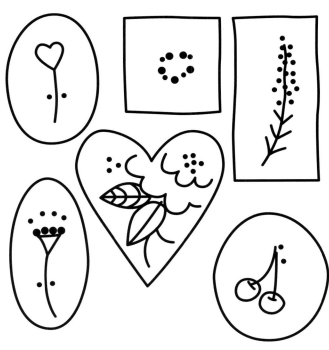

Summer Charm Pin

The Fairy Queen Pillow

W hen you're in the garden, look carefully at every bird that flies nearby. One may be carrying the fairy queen! She flits here and there, visiting her loyal subjects and sprinkling her fairy dust over their gardens. Yes, I'm about 12 years old at heart . . . can you tell?

FINISHED SIZE: 24" × 17" • **EMBROIDERY SIZE" 9" × 8"**

Made by Meg Hawkey

Materials

Yardage is based on 42"-wide fabric. Fat quarters measure 18" × 21". Check your supplies to see what you already have and what's needed.

Fabric and Supplies

1 fat quarter of cream solid for embroidery background

1 fat quarter of white muslin for embroidery backing

⅛ yard of white floral for inner border

⅛ yard of blue dot for middle border

½ yard of pink floral for outer border

⅝ yard of fabric for pillow back

24" length of 2½"-wide vintage crocheted lace edging

24" length of ¾"-wide pink rickrack

Color fixative

Embroidery needle, size 7 or 8

5"spring-tension embroidery hoop

8½" × 9½" piece of freezer paper

Polyester fiberfill for stuffing

Colored Pencils

Colors listed below are Prismacolor Premier Soft Core colored pencils.

Canary Yellow, PC916

Light Green, PC920

Pink, PC929

Beige, PC997

Blue Lake, PC1102

Caribbean Sea, PC1103

Goldenrod, PC1034

Beige Sienna, PC1080

Embroidery Floss

Colors listed at right are for Cosmo Shabon-dama metallic, Cosmo size 25, and Cosmo Seasons variegated 6-strand embroidery floss. Consult

the floss photos on page 12 when using other brands.

Yellow Iridescent (78-2) for fairy's crown and necklace

Pink Iridescent (78-4) for fairy's crown

Mauve Iridescent (78-5) for fairy's dress

Silver Iridescent (78-8) for fairy's wings

Gray (154) for bird's eye

Dark Blue (5022) for bird's head, wings, and tail

Brown (5029) for fairy's hair, bird's beak, and bird's feet

Ruby (8008) for fairy's mouth

Fuchsia (8009) for ribbon and bird's throat

Gold (8032) for bird's throat, breast, tail, and eye

Taupe (8039) for fairy's face, neck, hands, and legs

Brunette (9012) for fairy's eyelids

Cutting

All measurements include ¼" seam allowances.

From the cream solid, cut:
1 rectangle, 12" × 14"

From the white muslin, cut:
1 rectangle, 12" × 14"

From the white floral, cut:
2 strips, 1½" × 8½"
2 strips, 1½" × 11½"

From the blue dot, cut:
2 strips, 1" × 10½"
2 strips, 1" × 12½"

From the pink floral, cut:
2 strips, 6½" × 11½"
2 strips, 3½" × 24½"

From the fabric for pillow back, cut:
1 rectangle, 17½" × 24½"

Tracing and Tinting the Design

Refer to "General Instructions" on page 6 for in-depth information on tracing, tinting, and embroidering the design.

1 Use the brown Pigma pen to center and trace the pattern on page 79 onto the right side of the cream rectangle.

2 Using the colored pencils, color the design in the following order, referring to the photo on page 77 as needed.

- **Pink:** Shade the bird's throat and the ribbon; blend. Shade it further with Pink; blend.
- **Goldenrod:** Tint the fairy's hair, bird's beak, and bird's feet; blend.
- **Canary Yellow:** Tint the crown; blend.
- **Beige Sienna:** Shade the fairy dress very lightly and blend.
- **Beige:** Lightly shade the pale areas of the bird and the fairy's face, neck, hands, and legs; blend. Shade the tips of the last row of the bird's wing feathers; blend.

- **Pink:** Blush the fairy's cheeks a tiny bit; blend.
- **Caribbean Sea:** Using the photo of the bird (page 77) as a guide, shade all the blue areas. When you blend, work some of the blue into the beige areas where they meet on the wing feathers and the tail, diffusing the edges.
- **Blue Lake:** Shade all the blue areas; blend.
- The fairy's wings are shaded with a few different randomly placed colors. When they're blended it will make the wings look iridescent! Shade very lightly with Pink, Light Green, and Caribbean Sea; blend.

3 Apply fixative to the colored design. Let dry and then heat set. Baste the muslin rectangle to the wrong side of the cream rectangle.

Embroidering the Design

Use two strands of floss and the embroidery needle to stitch the design unless otherwise indicated.

- **Dark Blue:** Backstitch the bird's head, wings, and tail. Fly stitch details in the bird's wings.
- **Fuchsia:** Backstitch the ribbon and the bird's throat.
- **Taupe:** Backstitch the fairy's face, neck, hands, and legs.
- **Gold:** Backstitch the bird's throat, breast, tail, and around the eye.
- **Brown:** Backstitch the fairy's hair and the bird's beak and feet.
- **Gray:** Satin stitch the pupil of the bird's eye.
- **Ruby:** Use one strand to backstitch the fairy's mouth.
- **Mauve Iridescent:** Backstitch the fairy's dress.
- **Silver Iridescent:** Use one strand to backstitch the fairy's wings.
- **Yellow Iridescent:** Backstitch the fairy's crown and make two-wrap French knots for the necklace.
- **Pink Iridescent:** Make two-wrap French knots on the tips of the crown.
- **Brunette:** Make one stitch for each fairy eyelid.

Trimming the Embroidery

1 Refer to "Pressing the Finished Embroidery" on page 16 to press the embroidered rectangle.

2 Refer to "Trimming the Finished Piece" on page 16 to mark lines 1¼" from the bottom and left edges of the 8½" × 9½" piece of freezer paper.

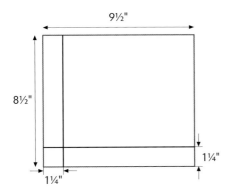

3 Place the freezer-paper template, shiny side down, on top of the embroidery. Line up the bird's beak with the left line and the bird's toes with the bottom line on the template. Press the template in place.

4 Trim the embroidery to 9½" × 8½", including seam allowances. Remove the freezer-paper template and press the embroidery again if needed.

Assembling the Pillow Top

Press the seam allowances as indicated by the arrows.

1 Sew white floral 1½" × 8½" strips to the short sides of the embroidery. Sew white floral 1½" × 11½" strips to the long sides of the embroidery. The pillow top should measure 11½" × 10½", including seam allowances.

2 Sew blue 1" × 10½" strips to the short sides of the pillow top. Sew blue 1" × 12½" strips to the long sides of the pillow top. The pillow top should measure 12½" × 11½", including seam allowances.

3 Sew pink floral 6½" × 11½" strips to the short sides of the pillow top.

4 Cut two 11½" lengths of lace. Pin the flat edge of the lace on the seamline between the blue and pink borders on each short end of the pillow top. Topstitch about ⅛" from the flat edge of the lace. Pin and sew the scalloped edge of the lace to the pink border.

5 Cut two 11½" lengths of rickrack. Pin the rickrack on top of the flat edge of the lace. Machine stitch a single line through the center of the rickrack. Trim the ends of the lace and rickrack if needed.

6 Sew pink floral 3½" × 24½" strips to the long sides of the pillow top. The pillow top should now measure 24½" × 17½".

Finishing the Pillow

1 Pin the pillow front on top of the 17½" × 24½" rectangle for the pillow back, right sides together. Sew around the perimeter of the pillow, leaving a 9" opening along the bottom edge for turning.

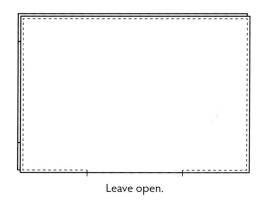

Leave open.

2 Turn the pillow right side out. Stuff firmly with fiberfill. Hand sew the opening closed.

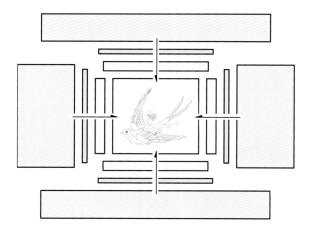

The Fairy Queen Pillow

About the Author

Always having a need to create, Meg Hawkey began quilting and hand embroidering as a child, using old quilts and vintage stitched pieces as her "instruction books." Years later, once her son became a teenager, she started working at a quilt shop, where she was encouraged to use her artwork to design embroidery patterns. That little push was all she needed to take a giant leap into the world of quilts, embroidery, and fabric design.

Meg's designs echo her love for nature and her whimsical sense of humor. Meg's color palette is as diverse as the subject matter of her designs. You'll find anything from delicate pastel florals to vibrant, bold colors. Everything belongs and all of it sings!

Visit Meg at the following places:

+ Website: CrabAppleHillStudio.com
+ Instagram: @meghawkey1
+ Facebook: @crabapplehillstudio
+ Pinterest: @crabapplehill

What's your creative passion?
Find it at ShopMartingale.com

books • eBooks • ePatterns • blog • free projects
videos • tutorials • inspiration • giveaways

Martingale®
Create with Confidence